I0170264

THE PROTOCOLS OF THE ELDERS OF ZION

IAP © 2009

Copyright © 2009 by IAP

All rights reserved. This publication is protected by Copyright and written permission should be obtained from the publisher prior to any prohibited reproduction, storage or transmission.

Printed in Scotts Valley, CA - USA.

Anonymous

The Protocols of the Elders of Zion /– 1st ed.

1. History

TABLE OF CONTENTS

INTRODUCTION

In History courses at Universities world-wide, Professors will tell you today this book was a forgery composed about 100 years ago. Richard Levy, an associate professor of history at the University of Illinois, Chicago, wrote that the *Protocols of the Elders of Zion* is one of the most important forgeries of modern times. Books such as *A Lie and a Libel, Warrant for Genocide: The Myth of the Jewish World-conspiracy and the Protocols f the Elders of Zion, Dismantling the Big Lie: The Protocols of the Elders of Zion, An Appraisal of the Protocols of Zion* and *The Truth about The Protocols of Zion* are just some of those that analyzed carefully this issue in the 20th century. Although this is out of question today to many scholars, this book is certainly still very important from the historical viewpoint. The Protocols might have been fabricated between 1895 and 1902 by Russian journalist Matvei Golovinski. According to Binjamin Segel, author of *A Lie and a Legel*, it was probably written between 1897 and 1899 in Paris, supervised by Pyotr Ivanovich Rachkovsky, head of the Russian secret police abroad. In his 4th publication of the Protocols in Russia, Nilus attributed them to Theodor Herzl, though. The fact is that nobody knows who really composed it.

The Protocols were first published in 1903 by Pavolachi (or Pavel) Krushevan, an instigator of the Kishinew pogrom, in his Russian newspaper called *Znamia*. In 1905 a longer version was published by Sergei Nilus. The first time it was published in English was in 1919 in England, but the references to Jews were replaced by Bolsheviks. In the United States, *The Dearborn Independent*, a newspaper controlled by Henry Ford, published lead articles about the "Jewish World Conspiracy" in 1920 and in Boston in the same year it appeared for the first time, in a Russian adaptation. Later, in 1927, Henry Ford would publicly retract and apologize for his publications.

In the 1920s, Victor Marsden, one of the *Morning Post[1]*'s reporters, translated the Protocols, which were published by an anti-Semitic organization known as the Britons. This edition we publish here is this one, the so-called Britons edition, but the British spelling was Americanized.

While in Germany, Alfred Rosenberg, the Nazi Party philosopher, published *The Protocols of the Elders of Zion and Jewish World Policy* in 1923, which was reprinted 3 times in a year, in the 1930s, in South Africa, the Protocols went on trial and it was officially declared a forgery.

In the 1920s and in the 1930s translations appeared in many countries, including France, Poland, Italy, Germany, Brazil etc.

In 1939, Hitler encouraged the distribution of *The Protocols* abroad to "reveal" the secret Jewish intention.

The Protocols were published in English through different titles, including: *Protocols of Zion, Protocols of the Wise Men of Zion, The Illuminati Protocols, Protocols of the Meetings of the Zionist Men of Wisdom, Protocols of the Learned Elders of Zion, The Protocols of the Elders of Zion* etc. The book is usually composed of 24, 25, 26 or 27 protocols. This translation presented here (The Britons) has 24.

Even though the text is about 100 years old and is considered a forgery by scholars today, it didn't just influenced politics in the past, but it still has some political influence in the present-day. Steven Jacobs and Mark Weitzman explain in their book *Dismantling the Big Lie* that the protocol book "has been wholeheartedly embraced in the Arab and Muslim world."

Finally, as Jacobs and Wetzman mention in their book, technological development, such as Internet, gave new life to the anti-Semitic beliefs, spread thanks to the protocols. Curiously, in 1993, in the Moscow court, a

---

[1] Conservative newspaper published in England from 1772 to 1937.

lawsuit asserted that the Protocols were part of a legitimate historical work, a surprisingly opposite result to the previous one provided by the South African court in the 1930s.

Fabio de Araujo, (Brazilian) Historian
Author of Mother Shipton: Secrets, Lies, and Prophecies

PROTOCOL 1

RIGHT LIES IN MIGHT. FREEDOM - AN IDEA ONLY. LIBERALISM. GOLD. FAITH. SELF-GOVERNMENT. DESPOTISM OF CAPITAL. THE INTERNAL FOE. THE MOB. ANARCHY. POLITICS VERSES JEW-MASONIC AUTHORITY. END JUSTIFIES MEANS. THE MOB A BLIND MAN. POLITICAL A.B.C. PARTY DISCORD. MOST SATISFACTORY FORM OF RULE-DESPOTISM. ALCOHOL. CLASSICISM. CORRUPTION. PRINCIPLES AND RULES OF THE JEW-MASONIC GOVERNMENT. TERROR. "LIBERTY, EQUALITY, FRATERNITY." PRINCIPLES OF DYNASTIC RULE. ANNIHILATION OF THE PRIVILEGES OF GOY-ARISTOCRACY (I.E., NON-JEW). ABSTRACTNESS OF "LIBERTY." POWER OF REMOVAL OF REPRESENTATIVES OF THE PEOPLE.

Putting aside fine phrases we shall speak of the significance of each thought: by comparisons and deductions we shall throw light upon surrounding facts.

What I am about to set forth, then, is our system from the two points of view, that of ourselves and that of the goyim (i.e., non-Jews).

It must be noted that men with bad instincts are more in number than the good, and therefore the best results in governing them are attained by violence and terrorization, and not by academic discussions. Every man aims at power, everyone would like to become a dictator if only he could, and rare indeed are the men who would not be willing to sacrifice the welfare of all for the sake of securing their own welfare.

What has restrained the beasts of prey who are called men? What has served for their guidance hitherto?

In the beginnings of the structure of society they were subjected to brutal and blind force; afterwards-to Law, which is the same force, only disguised. I draw the conclusion that by the law of nature right lies in force.

Political freedom is an idea but not a fact. This idea one must know how to apply whenever it appears necessary with this bait of an idea to attract the masses of the people to one's party for the purpose of crushing another who is in authority. This task is rendered easier if the opponent has himself been infected with the idea of freedom, SO-CALLED LIBERALISM, and, for the sake of an idea, is willing to yield some of his power. It is precisely here that the triumph of our theory appears: the slackened reins of government are immediately, by the law of life, caught up and gathered together by a new hand, because the blind might of the nation cannot for one single day exist without guidance, and the new author merely fits into the place of the old already weakened by liberalism.

In our day the power which has replaced that of the rulers who were liberal is the power of Gold. Time was when Faith ruled. The idea of freedom is impossible of realization because no one knows how to use it with moderation. It is enough to hand over a people to self-government for a certain length of time for that people to be turned into a disorganized mob. From that moment on we get internecine strife which soon develops into battles between classes, in the midst of which States burn down and their importance is reduced to that of a heap of ashes.

Whether a State exhausts itself in its own convulsions, whether its internal discord brings it under the power of external foes - in any case it can be accounted irretrievably lost: IT IS IN OUR POWER. The despotism of Capital, which is entirely in our hands, reaches out to it a straw that the State, willy-nilly, must take hold of: if not - it goes to the bottom.

Should anyone of a liberal mind say that such reactions as the above are immoral I would put the following questions - If every State has two foes and if in regard to the external foe it is allowed and not considered immoral to use every manner and art of conflict for example to keep the enemy in ignorance of plans of attack and defense, to attack him by night or in superior numbers, then in what way can the same means in regard to a worse foe the destroyer of the structure of society and the commonweal, be called immoral and not permissible?

Is it possible for any sound logical mind to hope with any success to guide crowds by the aid of reasonable counsels and arguments, when any objection or contradiction, senseless though it may be, can be made and when such objection may find more favor with the people, whose powers of reasoning are superficial? Men in masses and the men of the masses, being guided solely by petty passions, paltry beliefs, customs, traditions and sentimental theorism, fall a prey to party dissension, which hinders any kind of agreement even on the basis of a perfectly reasonable argument. Every resolution of a crowd depends upon a chance or packed majority which in its ignorance of political secrets puts forth some ridiculous resolution that lays in the administration a seed of anarchy.

The political has nothing in common with the moral. The ruler who is governed by the moral is not a skilled politician, and is therefore unstable on his throne. He who wishes to rule must have recourse both to cunning and to make-believe. Great national qualities, like frankness and honesty are vices in politics for they bring down rulers from their thrones more effectively and more certainly than the most powerful enemy. Such qualities must be the attributes of the kingdoms of the goyim, but we must in no wise be guided by them.

Our right lies in force. The word "right" is an abstract thought and proved by nothing. The word means no more than: -Give me what I want in order that thereby I might have a proof that I am stronger than you.

Where does right begin? Where does it end?

In any State in which there is a bad organization of authority, an impersonality of laws and of the rulers who have lost their personality amid the flood of rights ever multiplying out of liberalism, I find a new right - to attack by the right of the strong, and to scatter to the winds all existing forces of order and regulation, to reconstruct all institutions and to become the sovereign lord of those who have left to us the rights of their power by laying them down voluntarily in their liberalism.

Our power in the present tottering condition of all forms of power will be more invincible than any other, because it will remain invisible until the moment when it has gained such strength that no cunning can any longer undermine it.

Out of the temporary evil we are now compelled to commit will emerge the good of an unshakable rule, which will restore the regular course of the machinery of the national life, brought to naught by liberalism. The result justifies the means. Let us, however, in our plans, direct our attention not so much to what is good and moral as to what is necessary and useful.

Before us is a plan in which is laid down strategically the line from which we cannot deviate without running the risk of seeing the labor of many centuries brought to naught.

In order to elaborate satisfactory forms of action it is necessary to have regard to the rascality, the slackness, the instability of the mob, its lack of capacity to understand and respect the conditions of its own life, or its own welfare. It must be understood that the might of a mob is blind, senseless and unreasoning force ever at the mercy of a suggestion from any side. The blind cannot lead the blind without bringing them into the abyss; consequently, members of the mob, upstarts from the people even though they should be as a genius for wisdom, yet having no understanding of the political, cannot come forward as leaders of the mob without bringing the whole nation to ruin.

Only one trained from childhood for independent rule can have understanding of the words that can be made up of the political alphabet.

A people left to itself, i.e., to upstarts from its midst, brings itself to ruin by party dissension's excited by the pursuit of power and honors and disorders arising therefrom. Is it possible for the masses of the people calmly and without petty jealousies to form judgments, to deal with the affairs of the country, which cannot be mixed up with personal interests? Can they defend themselves from an eternal foe? It is unthinkable, for a plan broken up into as many parts as there are heads in the mob, loses all homogeneity, and thereby becomes unintelligible and impossible of execution.

It is only with a despotic ruler that plans can be elaborated extensively and clearly in such a way as to distribute the whole properly among the several parts of the machinery of the State: from this the conclusion is inevitable that a satisfactory form of government for any country is one that concentrates in the hands of one responsible person. Without an absolute despotism there can be no existence for civilization which is carried on not by the masses but by their guide, whosoever that person may be. The mob is a savage and displays its savagery at every opportunity.

The moment the mob seizes freedom in its hands it quickly turns to anarchy, which in itself is the highest degree of savagery.

Behold the alcoholized animals, bemused with drink, the right to an immoderate use of which comes along with freedom. It is not for us and ours to walk that road. The peoples of the goyim are bemused with alcoholic liquors; their youth has grown stupid on classicism and from early immorality, into which it has been inducted by our special agents - by tutors, lackeys, governesses in the houses of the wealthy, by clerks and others, by our women in the places of dissipation frequented by the goyim. In the number of these last I count also the so-called "society ladies," voluntary followers of the others in corruption and luxury.

Our countersign is -Force and Make-believe. Only force conquers in political affairs, especially if it be concealed in the talents essential to statesmen. Violence must be the principle, and cunning and make-believe the rule for governments which do not want to lay down their crowns at the feet of agents of some new power. This evil is the one and only means to attain the end, the good. Therefore we must not stop at bribery, deceit and treachery when they should serve towards the attainment of our end. In politics one must know how to seize the property of others without hesitation if by it we secure submission and sovereignty.

Our State, marching along the path of peaceful conquest, has the right to replace the horrors of war by less noticeable and more satisfactory sentences of death, necessary to maintain the terror which tends to produce blind submission. Just but merciless severity is the greatest factor of strength in the State: not only for the sake of gain but also in the name of duty, for the sake of victory, we must keep to the program of violence and make-believe. The doctrine of squaring accounts is precisely as strong as the means of which it makes use. Therefore it is not so much by the means themselves as by the doctrine of severity that we shall triumph and bring all governments into subjection to our super-government. It is enough for them to know that we are merciless for all disobedience to cease.

Far back in ancient times we were the first to cry among the masses of the people the words "Liberty, Equality, Fraternity," words many times repeated since those days by stupid poll-parrots who from all sides round flew down upon these baits and with them carried away the well-being of the world, true freedom of the individual, formerly so well guarded against the pressure of the mob. The would-be wise men of the goyim, the intellectuals, could not make anything out of the uttered words in their abstractness; did not note the contradiction of their meaning and inter-relation: did not see that in nature there is no equality, cannot be freedom: that Nature herself has established inequality of minds, of characters, and capacities, just as immutable as she has established subordination to her laws: never stopped to think that the mob is a blind thing, that upstarts elected from among it to bear rule are, in regard to the political, the same blind men as the mob itself, that the adept, though he be a fool, can yet rule, whereas the non-adept, even if he were a genius, understands nothing in the political - to all these things the goyim paid no regard; yet all the time it was based upon these things that dynastic rule rested: the father passed on to the son a knowledge of the course of political affairs in such wise that none should know it but members of the dynasty and none could betray it to the governed. As time went on the meaning of the dynastic transference of the true position of affairs in the political was lost, and this aided the success of our cause. In all corners of the earth the words "Liberty, Equality, Fraternity" brought to our ranks, thanks to our blind agents, whole legions who bore our banners with enthusiasm. And all the time these words were canker-worms at work boring into the well-being of the goyim, putting an end everywhere to peace, quiet, solidarity and destroying all the foundations of the goy States. As you will see later this helped us to our triumph; it gave us the possibility, among other things, of getting into our hands the master card - the destruction of the privileges, or in other words of the very existence of the aristocracy of the goyim, that c ass which was the only defense peoples and countries had against us. On the ruins of the natural and genealogical aristocracy of the goyim we have set up the aristocracy of our educated class headed by the aristocracy of money. The qualifications for this aristocracy we have established in wealth, which is dependent upon us and in knowledge, for which our learned elders provide the motive force.

Our triumph has been rendered easier by the fact that in our relations with the men whom we wanted we have always worked upon the most sensitive chords of the human mind, upon the cash account, upon the cupidity, upon the insatiability for material needs of man; and each one of these human weaknesses, taken alone, is sufficient to paralyze initiative for it hands over the will of men to the disposition of him who has bought their activities.

The abstraction of freedom has enabled us to persuade the mob in all countries that their government is nothing but the steward of the people who are the owners of the country, and that the steward may be replaced like a worn-out glove.

It is this possibility of replacing the representatives of the people which has placed them at our disposal, and, as it were, given us the power of appointment.

16

PROTOCOL 2

ECONOMIC WARS - THE FOUNDATION OF THE JEWISH
PREDOMINANCE. FIGURE-HEAD GOVERNMENT AND "SECRET
ADVISORS." SUCCESS OF DESTRUCTIVE DOCTRINES.
ADAPTABILITY IN POLITICS. PART PLAYED BY THE PRESS.
COST OF GOLD AND VALUE OF JEWISH SACRIFICE.

It is indispensable for our purpose that wars, so far as possible, should not result in territorial gains: war will thus be brought on to the economic ground, where the nations will not fail to perceive in the assistance we give the strength of our predominance, and this state of things will put both sides at the mercy of our international agentur[2]; which possesses millions of eyes ever on the watch and unhampered by any limitations whatsoever. Our international rights will then wipe out national rights, in the proper sense of right, and will rule the nations precisely as the civil law of States rules the relations of their subjects among themselves.

The administrators, whom we shall choose from among the public, with strict regard to their capacities for servile obedience, will not be persons trained in the arts of government, and will therefore easily become pawns in our game in the hands of men of learning and genius who will be their advisers, specialists bred and reared from early childhood to rule the affairs of the whole world. As is well known to you, these specialists of ours have been drawing to fit them for rule the information they need from our political plans, from the lessons of history, from observations made of the events of every moment as it passes. The goyim are not guided by practical use of unprejudiced historical observation, but by theoretical routine without any critical regard for consequent results. We need not, therefore, take any account of them - let them amuse themselves until the hour strikes, or live on hopes of new forms of enterprising pastime, or on the memories of all they have enjoyed. For them let that play the

---

[2] agency

17

principal part which we have persuaded them to accept as the dictates of science (theory). It is with this object in view that we are constantly, by means of our press, arousing a blind confidence in these theories. The intellectuals of the goyim will puff themselves up with their knowledge and without any logical verification of it will put into effect all the information available from science, which our AGENTUR specialists have cunningly pieced together for the purpose of educating their minds in the direction we want.

Do not suppose for a moment that these statements are empty words: think carefully of the successes we arranged for Darwinism, Marxism, Nietzsche-ism. To us Jews, at any rate, it should be plain to see what a disintegrating importance these directives have had upon the minds of the goyim.

It is indispensable for us to take account of the thoughts, characters, tendencies of the nations in order to avoid making slips in the political and in the direction of administrative affairs. The triumph of our system, of which the component parts of the machinery may be variously disposed according to the temperament of the peoples met on our way, will fail of success if the practical application of it be not based upon a summing up of the lessons of the past in the light of the present.

In the hands of the States of to-day there is a great force that creates the movement of thought in the people, and that is the Press. The part played by the Press is to keep pointing out requirements supposed to be indispensable, to give voice to the complaints of the people, to express and to create discontent. It is in the Press that the triumph of freedom of speech finds its incarnation. But the goyim States have not known how to make use of this force; and it has fallen into our hands. Through the Press we have gained the power to influence while remaining ourselves in the shade; thanks to the Press we have got the gold in our hands, notwithstanding that we have had to gather it out of oceans of blood and tears. But it has paid us, though we have sacrificed many of our people. Each victim on our side is worth in the sight of God a thousand goyim.

PROTOCOL 3

Today I may tell you that our goal is now only a few steps off. There remains a small space to cross and the whole long path we have trodden is ready now to close its cycle of the Symbolic Snake, by which we symbolize our people. When this ring closes, all the States of Europe will be locked in its coil as in a powerful vice.

The constitution scales of these days will shortly break down, for we have established them with a certain lack of accurate balance in order that they may oscillate incessantly until they wear through the pivot on which they turn. The goyim are under the impression that they have welded them sufficiently strong and they have all along kept on expecting that the scales would come into equilibrium. But the pivots - the kings on their thrones - are hemmed in by their representatives, who play the fool, distraught with their own uncontrolled and irresponsible power. This power they owe to the terror which has been breathed into the palaces. As they have no meant of getting at their people, into their very midst, the kings on their thrones are no longer able to come to terms with them and so strengthen themselves against seekers after power. We have made a gulf between the farseeing sovereign Power and the blind force of the people so that both have lost all meaning, for like the blind man and his stick, both are powerless apart.

In order to incite seekers after power to a misuse of power we have set all forces in opposition one to another, breaking up their liberal tendencies towards independence. To this end we have stirred up every form of enterprise, we have armed all parties, we have set up authority as a target for every ambition. Of States we have made gladiatorial arenas where a host of confused issues contend....A little more, and disorders and bankruptcy will be universal....

Babblers inexhaustible have turned into oratorical contests the sittings of Parliament and Administrative Boards. Bold journalists and unscrupulous pamphleteers daily fall upon executive officials. Abuses of power will put the final touch in preparing all institutions for their overthrow and everything will fly skyward under the blows of the maddened mob.

All people are chained down to heavy toil by poverty more firmly than ever they were chained by slavery and serfdom; from these, one way and another, they might free themselves, these could be settled with, but from want they will never get away. We have included in the constitution such rights as to the masses appear fictitious and not actual rights. All these so-called "People's Rights" can exist only in idea, an idea which can never be realized in practical life. What is it to the proletariat laborer, bowed double over his heavy toil, crushed by his lot in life, if talkers get the right to babble, if journalists get the right to scribble any nonsense side by side with good stuff, once the proletariat has no other profit out of the constitution save only those pitiful crumbs which we fling them from our table in return for their voting in favor of what we dictate, in favor of the men we place in power, the servants of our AGENTUR.... Republican right for a poor man are no more than a bitter piece of irony for the necessity he is under of toiling almost all day gives him no present use of them, but on the other hand robs him of all guarantee of regular and certain earnings by making him dependent on strikes by his comrades or lockouts by his masters.

The people under our guidance have annihilated the aristocracy, who were their one and only defense and foster-mother for the sake of their own advantage which is inseparably bound up with the well-being of the people. Nowadays, with the destruction of the aristocracy, the people have fallen into the grips of merciless money-grinding scoundrels who have laid a pitiless and cruel yoke upon the necks of the workers.

We appear on the scene as alleged saviors of the worker from this oppression when we propose to him to enter the ranks of our fighting forces - Socialists, Anarchists, Communists - to whom we always give rapport in accordance with an alleged brotherly rule (of the solidarity of all humanity) of our SOCIAL MASONRY. The aristocracy, which enjoyed by law the labor of the workers, was interested in seeing that the workers were well fed, healthy and strong. We are interested in just the opposite - in the diminution, the KILLING OUT OF THE GOYIM. Our power is in the chronic shortness of food and physical weakness of the worker because by all that this implies he is made the slave of our will, and he will not find in his own authorities either strength or energy to set against our will. Hunger creates the right of capital to rule the worker more surely than it was given to the aristocracy by the legal authority of kings.

By want and the envy and hatred which it engenders we shall move the mobs and with their hands we shall wipe out all those who hinder on our way.

WHEN THE HOUR STRIKES FOR OUR SOVEREIGN LORD OF ALL THE WORLD TO BE CROWNED IT IS THESE SAME HANDS WHICH WILL SWEEP AWAY EVERYTHING THAT MIGHT BE A HINDRANCE THERETO.

The goyim have lost the habit of thinking unless prompted by the suggestions of our specialists. Therefore they do not see the urgent necessity of what we, when our kingdom comes, shall adopt all at once, namely this, that IT IS ESSENTIAL TO TEACH IN NATIONAL SCHOOLS ONE SIMPLE, TRUE PIECE OF KNOWLEDGE, THE BASIS OF ALL KNOWLEDGE - THE KNOWLEDGE OF THE

STRUCTURE OF HUMAN LIFE, OF SOCIAL EXISTENCE, WHICH REQUIRES DIVISION OF LABOUR, AND, CONSEQUENTLY, THE DIVISION OF MEN INTO CLASSES AND CONDITIONS. It is essential for all to know that owing to DIFFERENCE IN THE OBJECTS OF HUMAN ACTIVITY THERE CANNOT BE ANY EQUALITY, that he who by any act of his compromises a whole class cannot be equally responsible before the law with him who affects no one but only his own honor. The true knowledge of the structure of society, into the secrets of which we do not admit the goyim, would demonstrate to all men that the positions and work must be kept within a certain circle, that they may not become a source of human suffering, arising from an education which does not correspond with the work which individuals are called upon to do. After a thorough study of this knowledge the peoples will voluntarily submit to authority and accept such position as is appointed them in the State. In the present state of knowledge and the direction we have given to its development the people, blindly believing things in print - cherishes - thanks to promptings intended to mislead and to its own ignorance a blind hatred towards all conditions which it considers above itself, for it has no understanding of the meaning of class and condition.

This hatred will be still further magnified by the effects of an ECONOMIC CRISIS, which will stop dealings on the exchanges and bring industry to a standstill. We shall create by all the secret subterranean methods open to us and with the aid of gold, which is all in our hands, A UNIVERSAL ECONOMIC CRISIS WHEREBY WE SHALL THROW UPON THE STREETS WHOLE MOBS OF WORKERS SIMULTANEOUSLY IN ALL THE COUNTRIES OF EUROPE. These mobs will rush delightedly to shed the blood of those whom, in the simplicity of their ignorance, they have envied from their cradles, and whose property they will then be able to loot.

"OURS" THEY WILL NOT TOUCH, BECAUSE THE MOMENT OF ATTACK WILL BE KNOWN TO US AND WE SHALL TAKE MEASURES TO PROTECT OUR OWN.

We have demonstrated that progress will bring all the goyim to the sovereignty of reason. Our despotism will be precisely that; for it will know how by wise severities to pacify all unrest, to cauterize liberalism out of all institutions.

When the populace has seen that all sorts of concessions and indulgences are yielded it in the name of freedom it has imagined itself to be sovereign lord and has stormed its way to power, but, naturally, like every other blind man it has come upon a host of stumbling blocks, IT HAS RUSHED TO FIND A GUIDE, IT HAS NEVER HAD THE SENSE TO RETURN TO THE FORMER STATE and it has laid down its plenipotentiary powers at OUR feet. Remember the French Revolution, to which it was we who gave the name of "Great": the secrets of its preparations are well known to us for it was wholly the work of our hands.

Ever since that time we have been leading the peoples from one disenchantment to another, so that in the end they should turn also from us in favor of that KING-DESPOT OF THE BLOOD OF ZION, WHOM WE ARE PREPARING FOR THE WORLD.

At the present day we are, as an international force, invincible, because if attacked by some we are supported by other States. It is the bottomless rascality of the goyim peoples, who crawl on their bellies to force, but are merciless towards weakness, unsparing to faults and indulgent to crimes, unwilling to bear the contradictions of a free social system but patient unto martyrdom under the violence of a bold despotism - it is those qualities which are aiding us to independence. From the premier-dictators of the present day the goyim peoples suffer patiently and bear such abuses as for the least of them they would have beheaded twenty kings.

What is the explanation of this phenomenon, this curious inconsequence of the masses of the peoples in their attitude towards what would appear to be events of the same order?

It is explained by the fact that these dictators whisper to the peoples through their agents that through these abuses they are inflicting injury on the States with the highest purpose - to secure the welfare of the peoples, the international brotherhood of them all, their solidarity and equality of rights. Naturally they do not tell the peoples that this unification must be accomplished only under our sovereign rule.

And thus the people condemn the upright and acquit the guilty, persuaded ever more and more that it can do whatsoever it wishes. Thanks to this state of things the people are destroying every kind of stability and creating disorders at every step.

The word "freedom" brings out the communities of men to fight against every kind of force, against every kind of authority, even against God and the laws of nature. For this reason we, when we come into our kingdom, shall have to erase this word from the lexicon of life as implying a principle of brute force which turns mobs into bloodthirsty beasts.

These beasts, it is true, fall asleep again every time when they have drunk their fill of blood, and at such times can easily be riveted into their chains. But if they be not given blood they will not sleep and continue to struggle.

PROTOCOL 4

Every republic passes through several stages. The first of these is comprised in the early days of mad raging by the blind mob, tossed hither and thither, right and left: the second is demagogy, from which is born anarchy, and that leads inevitably to despotism - not any longer legal and overt, and therefore responsible despotism, but to unseen and secretly hidden, yet nevertheless sensibly felt despotism in the hands of some secret organization or other, whose acts are the more unscrupulous inasmuch as it works behind a screen, behind the backs of all sorts of agents, the changing of whom not only does not injuriously affect but actually aids the secret force by saving it, thanks to continual changes, from the necessity of expending its resources on the rewarding of long services.

Who and what is in a position to overthrow an invisible force? And this is precisely what our force is. Gentile masonry blindly serves as a screen for us and our objects, both the plan of action of our force, even its very abiding-place, remains for the whole people an unknown mystery.

But even freedom might be harmless and have its place in the State economy without injury to the well-being of the peoples if it rested upon the foundation of faith in God, upon the brotherhood of humanity, unconnected with the conception of equality, which is negated by the very laws of creation, for they have established subordination. With such a faith as this a people might be governed by a wardship of parishes, and would walk contentedly and humbly under the guiding hand of its spiritual pastor submitting to the dispositions of God upon earth. This is the reason why IT IS INDISPENSABLE FOR US TO UNDERMINE ALL FAITH, TO TEAR OUT OF THE MINDS OF THE GOYIM THE VERY

PRINCIPLE OF GODHEAD AND THE SPIRIT, AND TO PUT IN ITS PLACE ARITHMETICAL CALCULATIONS AND MATERIAL NEEDS.

In order to give the goyim no time to think and take note, their minds must be diverted towards industry and trade. Thus, all the nations will be swallowed up in the pursuit of gain and in the race for it will not take note of their common foe. But again, in order that freedom may once for all disintegrate and ruin the communities of the goyim, we must put industry on a speculative basis: the result of this will be that what is withdrawn from the land by industry will slip through the hands and pass into speculation, that is, to our classes.

The intensified struggle for superiority and shocks delivered to economic life will create, nay, have already created, disenchanted, cold and heartless communities. Such communities will foster a strong aversion towards the higher political and towards religion. Their only guide is gain, that is Gold, which they will erect into a veritable cult, for the sake of those material delights which it can give. Then will the hour strike when, not for the sake of attaining the good, not even to win wealth, but solely out of hatred towards the privileged, the lower classes of the goyim will follow our lead against our rivals for power, the intellectuals of the goyim.

PROTOCOL 5

CREATION OF AN INTENSIFIED CENTRALIZED OF
GOVERNMENT. METHODS OF SEIZING POWER BY MASONRY.
CAUSES OF THE IMPOSSIBILITY OF AGREEMENT BETWEEN
STATES. THE STATE OF "PREDESTINATION" OF THE JEWS.
GOLD - THE ENGINE OF THE MACHINERY OF STATES.
SIGNIFICANCE OF PERSONAL INITIATIVE. THE SUPER-
GOVERNMENT.

What form of administrative rule can be given to communities in which corruption has penetrated everywhere, communities where riches are attained only by the clever surprise tactics of semi-swindling tricks; where looseness reigns: where morality is maintained by penal measures and harsh laws but not by voluntary accepted principles: where the feelings towards faith and country are obliterated by cosmopolitan convictions? What form of rule is to be given to these communities if not that despotism which I shall describe to you later? We shall create an intensified centralization of government in order to grip in our hands all the forces of the community. We shall regulate mechanically all the actions of the political life of our subjects by new laws. These laws will withdraw one by one all the indulgences and liberties which have been permitted by the goyim, and our kingdom will be distinguished by a despotism of such magnificent proportions as to be at any moment and in every place in a position to wipe out any goyim who oppose us by deed or word.

We shall be told that such a despotism as I speak of is not consistent with the progress of these days, but I will prove to you that it is.

In the times when the peoples looked upon kings on their thrones as on a pure manifestation of the will of God, they submitted without a murmur to the despotic power of kings: but from the day when we insinuated into their minds the conception of their own rights they began to regard the occupants of thrones as mere ordinary mortals. The holy unction of the

Lord's Anointed has fallen from the heads of kings in the eyes of the people, and when we also robbed them of their faith in God the might of power was flung upon the streets into the place of public proprietorship and was seized by us.

Moreover, the art of directing masses and individuals by means of cleverly manipulated theory and verbiage, by regulations of life in common and all sorts of other quirks, in all which the goyim understand nothing, belongs likewise to the specialists of our administrative brain. Reared on analysis, observation, on delicacies of fine calculation, in this species of skill we have no rivals, any more than we have either in the drawing up of plans of political actions and solidarity. In this respect the Jesuits alone might have compared with us, but we have contrived to discredit them in the eyes of the unthinking mob as an overt organization, while we ourselves all the while have kept our secret organization in the shade. However, it is probably all the same to the world who is its sovereign lord, whether the head of Catholicism or our despot of the blood of Zion! But to us, the Chosen People, it is very far from being a matter of indifference.

FOR A TIME PERHAPS WE MIGHT BE SUCCESSFULLY DEALT WITH BY A COALITION OF THE GOYIM OF ALL THE WORLD: but from this danger we are secured by the discord existing among them whose roots are so deeply seated that they can never now be plucked up. We have set one against another the personal and national reckonings of the goyim, religious and race hatreds, which we have fostered into a huge growth in the course of the past twenty centuries. This is the reason why there is not one State which would anywhere receive support if it were to raise its arm, for every one of them must bear in mind that any agreement against us would be unprofitable to itself. We are too strong - there is no evading our power. THE NATIONS CANNOT COME TO EVEN AN INCONSIDERABLE PRIVATE AGREEMENT WITHOUT OUR SECRETLY HAVING A HAND IN IT.

PER ME REGES REGNANT. "It is through Me that Kings reign." And it was said by the prophets that we were chosen by God Himself to rule over the whole earth. God has endowed us with genius that we may be equal to our task. Were genius in the opposite camp it would still struggle against us, but even so a newcomer is no match for the old established settler: the struggle would be merciless between us, such a fight as the world has never yet seen. Aye, and the genius on their side would have arrived too late. All the wheels of the machinery of all States go by the force of the engine, which is in our hands, and that engine of the machinery of States is - Gold. The science of political economy invented by our learned elders has for long past been giving royal prestige to capital. Capital, if it is to co-operate untrammeled, must be free to establish a monopoly of industry and trade: this is already being put in execution by an unseen hand in all quarters of the world. This freedom will give political force to those engaged in industry, and that will help to oppress the people. Nowadays it is more important to disarm the peoples than to lead them into war: more important to use for our advantage the passions which have burst into flames than to quench their fire: more important to catch up and interpret the ideas of others to suit ourselves than to eradicate them. THE PRINCIPAL OBJECT OF OUR DIRECTORATE CONSISTS IN THIS: TO DEBILITATE THE PUBLIC MIND BY CRITICISM TO LEAD IT AWAY FROM SERIOUS REFLECTIONS CALCULATED TO AROUSE RESISTANCE TO DISTRACT THE FORCES OF THE MIND TOWARDS A SHAM FIGHT OF EMPTY ELOQUENCE.

In all ages the peoples of the world, equally with individuals, have accepted words for deeds, for THEY ARE CONTENT WITH A SHOW and rarely pause to note, in the public arena, whether promises are followed by performance. Therefore we shall establish show institutions which will give eloquent proof of their benefit to progress.

We shall assume to ourselves the liberal physiognomy of all parties, of all directions, and we shall give that physiognomy a voice IN ORATORS WHO WILL SPEAK SO MUCH THAT THEY WILL EXHAUST THE PATIENCE OF THEIR HEARERS AND PRODUCE AN ABHORRENCE OF ORATORY.

IN ORDER TO PUT PUBLIC OPINION INTO OUR HANDS WE MUST BRING IT INTO A STATE OF BEWILDERMENT BY GIVING EXPRESSION FROM ALL SIDES TO SO MANY CONTRADICTORY OPINIONS AND FOR SUCH LENGTH OF

TIME AS WILL SUFFICE TO MAKE THE GOYIM LOSE THEIR HEADS IN THE LABYRINTH AND COME TO SEE THAT THE BEST THING IS TO HAVE NO OPINION OF ANY KIND IN MATTERS POLITICAL, which it is not given to the public to understand, because they are understood only by him who guides the public. This is the first secret.

The second secret requisite for the success of our government is comprised in the following. To multiply to such an extent national failings, habits, passions, conditions of civil life, that it will be impossible for anyone to know where he is in the resulting chaos, so that the people in consequence will fail to understand one another. This measure will also serve us in another way, namely, to sow discord in all parties, to dislocate all collective forces which are still unwilling to submit to us, and to discourage any kind of personal initiative which might in any degree hinder our affair. THERE IS NO- THING MORE DANGEROUS THAN PERSONAL INITIATIVE; if it has genius behind it, such initiative can do more than can be done by millions of people among whom we have sown discord. We must so direct the education of the goyim communities that whenever they come upon a matter requiring initiative they may drop their hands in despairing impotence. The strain which results from freedom of action saps the forces when it meets with the freedom of another. From this collision arise grave moral shocks, disenchantments, failures. BY ALL THESE MEANS WE SHALL SO WEAR DOWN THE GOYIM THAT THEY WILL BE COMPELLED TO OFFER US INTERNATIONAL POWER A NATURE THAT BY ITS POSITION WILL ENABLE US WITHOUT ANY VIOLENCE GRADUALLY TO ABSORB ALL THE STATE FORCES OF THE WORLD AND TO FORM A SUPER-GOVERNMENT. In place of the rulers of to-day we shall set up a bogey which will be called the Super-Government Administration. Its hands will reach out in all directions like nippers and its organization will be of such colossal dimensions that it cannot fail to subdue all the nations of the world.

PROTOCOL 6

MONOPOLITIES; UPON THEM DEPEND THE FORTUNES OF THE GOYIM. TAKING OF THE LAND OUT OF HANDS OF THE ARISTOCRACY. TRADE, INDUSTRY AND SPECULATION. LUXURY. RISE OF WAGES AND INCREASE OF PRICE IN THE ARTICLES OF PRIMARY NECESSITY. ANARCHISM AND DRUNKENESS. SECRET MEANING OF THE OF THE PROPAGANDA OF ECONOMIC THEORIES.

We shall soon begin to establish huge monopolies, reservoirs of colossal riches, upon which even large fortunes of the goyim will depend to such an extent that they will go to the bottom together with the credit of the States on the day after the political smash....

You gentlemen here present who are economists, just strike an estimate of the significance of this combination !

In every possible way we must develop the significance of our Super-Government by representing it as the Protector and Benefactor of all those who voluntarily submit to us.

The aristocracy of the goyim as a political force, is dead - we need not take it into account; but as landed proprietors they can still be harmful to us from the fact that they are self-sufficing in the resources upon which they live. It is essential therefore for us at whatever cost to deprive them of their land. This object will be best attained by increasing the burdens upon landed property - in loading lands with debts. These measures will check land-holding and keep it in a state of humble and unconditional submission.

The aristocrats of the goyim, being hereditarily incapable of contenting themselves with little, will rapidly burn up and fizzle out.

At the same time we must intensively patronize trade and industry, but, first and foremost, speculation, the part played by which is to provide a counterpoise to industry: the absence of speculative industry will multiply capital in private hands and will serve to restore agriculture by freeing the land from indebtedness to the land banks. What we want is that industry should drain off from the land both labor and capital and by means of speculation transfer into our hands all the money of the world, and thereby throw all the goyim into the ranks of the proletariat. Then the goyim will bow down before us, if for no other reason but to get the right to exist.

To complete the ruin of the industry of the goyim we shall bring to the assistance of speculation the luxury which we have developed among the goyim, that greedy demand for luxury which is swallowing up everything. WE SHALL RAISE THE RATE OF WAGES, HOWEVER, WILL NOT BRING ANY ADVANTAGE TO THE WORKERS, FOR, AT THE SAME TIME, WE SHALL PRODUCE A RISE IN PRICES OF THE FIRST NECESSARIES OF LIFE, ALLEGING THAT IT ARISES FROM THE DECLINE OF AGRICULTURE AND CATTLE-BREEDING: WE SHALL FURTHER UNDERMINE ARTFULLY AND DEEPLY SOURCES OF PRODUCTION, BY ACCUSTOMING THE WORKERS TO ANARCHY AND TO DRUNKENNESS AND SIDE BY SIDE THEREWITH TAKING ALL MEASURE TO EXTIRPATE FROM THE FACE OF THE EARTH ALL THE EDUCATED FORCES OF THE GOYIM.

IN ORDER THAT THE TRUE MEANING OF THINGS MAY NOT STRIKE THE GOYIM BEFORE THE PROPER TIME WE SHALL MASK IT UNDER AN ALLEGED ARDENT DRIVE TO SERVE THE WORKING CLASSES AND THE GREAT PRINCIPLES OF POLITICAL ECONOMY ABOUT WHICH OUR ECONOMIC THEORIES ARE CARRYING ON AN ENERGETIC PROPAGANDA.

PROTOCOL 7

OBJECT OF THE INTENSIFICATION OF ARMAMENTS. FERMENTS, DISCORDS AND HOSTILITY ALL OVER THE WORLD. CHECKING THE OPPOSITION OF THE GOYIM BY WARS AND BY A UNIVERSAL WAR. SECRECY MEANS SUCCESS IN THE POLITICAL. THE PRESS AND PUBLIC OPINION. THE GUNS OF AMERICA, CHINA AND JAPAN.

The intensification of armaments, the increase of police forces - are all essential for the completion of the aforementioned plans. What we have to get at is that there should be in all the States of the world, besides ourselves, only the masses of the proletariat, a few millionaires devoted to our interests, police and soldiers. Throughout all Europe, and by means of relations with Europe, in other continents also, we must create ferments, discords and hostility. Therein we gain a double advantage. In the first place we keep in check all countries, for they well know that we have the power whenever we like to create disorders or to restore order. All these countries are accustomed to see in us an indispensable force of coercion. In the second place, by our intrigues we shall tangle up all the threads which we have stretched into the cabinets of all States by means of politics, by economic treaties, or loan obligations. In order to succeed in this we must use great cunning and penetration during negotiations and agreements, but, as regards what is called the "official language," we shall keep to the opposite tactics and assume the mask of honesty and compliancy. In this way the peoples and governments of the goyim, whom we have taught to look only at the outside of whatever we present to their notice, will still continue to accept us as the benefactors and saviors of the human race.

We must be in a position to respond to every act of opposition by war with the neighbors of that country which dares to oppose us: but if these neighbors should also venture to stand collectively together against us, then we must offer resistance by a universal war.

The principal factor of success in the political is the secrecy of its undertakings: the word should not agree with the deeds of the diplomat.

We must compel the governments of the goyim to take action in the direction favored by our widely conceived plan, already approaching the desired consummation, by what we shall represent as public opinion, secretly prompted by us through the means of that so-called "Great Power" -- THE PRESS, WHICH, WITH A FEW EXCEPTIONS THAT MAY BE DISREGARDED, IS ALREADY ENTIRELY IN OUR HANDS.

In a word, to sum up our system of keeping the governments of the goyim in Europe in check, we shall show our strength to one of them by terrorist attempts and to all, if we allow the possibility of a general rising against us, we shall respond with the guns of America or China or Japan.

Protocol 8

Ambiguous employment of juridical right. Assistants of the Masonic directorate. Special school and super-educational training. Economists and millionaires. To whom to entrust responsible post in the government.

We must arm ourselves with all the weapons which our opponents might employ against us. We must search out in the very finest shades of expression and the knotty points of the lexicon of law justification for those cases where we shall have to pronounce judgments that might appear abnormally audacious and unjust, for it is important that these resolutions should be set forth in expressions that shall seem to be the most exalted moral principles cast into legal form. Our directorate must surround itself with all these forces of civilization among which it will have to work. It will surround itself with publicists, practical jurists, administrators, diplomats and, finally, with persons prepared by a special super-educational training IN OUR SPECIAL SCHOOLS. These persons will have cognizance of all the secrets of the social structure, they will know all the languages that can be made up by political alphabets and words; they will be made acquainted with the whole underside of human nature, with all its sensitive chords on which they will have to play. These chords are the cast of mind of the goyim, their tendencies, shortcomings, vices and qualities, the particularities of classes and conditions. Needless to say that the talented assistants of authority, of whom I speak, will be taken not from among the goyim, who are accustomed to perform their administrative work without giving themselves the trouble to think what its aim is, and never consider what it is needed for. The administrators of the goyim sign papers without reading them, and they serve either for mercenary reasons or from ambition.

We shall surround our government with a whole world of economists.

That is the reason why economic sciences form the principal subject of the teaching given to the Jews. Around us again will be a whole constellation of bankers, industrialists, capitalists and - THE MAIN THING - MILLIONAIRES, BECAUSE IN SUBSTANCE EVERYTHING WILL BE SETTLED BY THE QUESTION OF FIGURES. For a time, until there will no longer be any risk in entrusting responsible posts in our States to our brother-Jews we shall put them in the hands of persons whose past and reputation are such that between them and the people lies an abyss, persons who, in case of disobedience to our instructions, must face criminal charges or disappear -- this in order to make them defend our interest to their last gasp.

PROTOCOL 9

APPLICATION OF MASONIC PRINCIPLES IN THE MATTER OF EDUCATING THE PEOPLES. MASONIC WATCHWORD. MEANING OF ANTI-SEMITISM. DICTATORSHIP OF MASONRY. TERROR. WHO ARE THE SERVANTS OF MASONRY. MEANING OF THE "CLEAR-SIGHTED" AND THE "BLIND" FORCES OF THE "GOYIM" STATES. COMMUNION BETWEEN AUTHORITY AND MOB. LICENSE OF LIBERALISM. SEIZURE OF EDUCATION AND TRAINING. FALSE THEORIES. INTERPRETATION OF LAWS. THE "UNDERGROUNDS" (METROPOLITANS).

In applying our principles let attention be paid to the character of the people in whose country you live and act; a general, identical application of them, until such time as the people shall have been re-educated to our pattern, cannot have success. But by approaching their application cautiously you will see that not a decade will pass before the most stubborn character will change and we shall add a new people to the ranks of those already subdued by us.

The words of the liberal, which are in effect the words of our freemasonic watchword, namely, "Liberty, Equality, Fraternity," will, when we come into our kingdom, be changed by us into words no longer of a watchword, but only an expression of idealism, namely, into: "The right of liberty, the duty of equality, the ideal of brotherhood." That is how we shall put it, and so we shall catch the bull by the horns... DE FACTO we have already wiped out every kind of rule except our own, although DE JURE there still remain a good many of them. Nowadays, if any States raise a protest against us it is only PRO FORMA at our discretion and by our direction, for THEIR ANTI-SEMITISM IS INDISPENSABLE TO US FOR THE MANAGEMENT OF OUR LESSER BRETHREN. I will not enter into further explanations, for this matter has formed the subject of repeated discussions amongst us.

For us there are no checks to limit the range of our activity. Our Super-

Government subsists in extra-legal conditions which are described in the accepted terminology by the energetic and forcible word - Dictatorship. I am in a position to tell you with a clear conscience that at the proper time we, the law-givers shall execute judgment and sentence, we shall slay and we shall spare, we, as head of all our troops, are mounted on the steed of the leader. We rule by force of will, because in our hands are the fragments of a once powerful party, now vanquished by us. AND THE WEAPONS IN OUR HANDS ARE LIMITLESS AMBITIONS, BURNING GREEDINESS, MERCILESS VENGEANCE, HATREDS AND MALICE.

IT IS FROM US THAT ALL-ENGULFING TERROR PROCEEDS. WE HAVE IN OUR SERVICE PERSONS OF ALL OPINIONS, OF ALL DOCTRINES, RESTORATING MONARCHISTS, DEMAGOGUES, SOCIALISTS, COMMUNISTS, AND UTOPIAN DREAMERS OF EVERY KIND. We have harnessed them all to the task: EACH ONE OF THEM ON HIS OWN ACCOUNT IS BORING AWAY AT THE LAST REMNANTS OF AUTHORITY, IS STRIVING TO OVERTHROW ALL ESTABLISHED FORM OF ORDER. By these acts all States are in torture; they exhort to tranquility, are ready to sacrifice everything for peace: but we will not give them peace until they openly acknowledge our international Super-Government, and with submissiveness.

The people have raised a howl about the necessity of settling the question of Socialism by way of an international agreement. DIVISION INTO FRACTIONAL PARTIES HAS GIVEN THEM INTO OUR HANDS, FOR, IN ORDER TO CARRY ON A CONTESTED STRUGGLE ONE MUST HAVE MONEY, AND THE MONEY IS ALL IN OUR HANDS.

We might have reason to apprehend a union between the "clear-sighted" force of the goy kings on their thrones and the "blind" force of the goy mobs, but we have taken all the needful measure against any such possibility: between the one and the other force we have erected a bulwark in the shape of a mutual terror between them. In this way the blind force of the people remains our support and we, and we only, shall provide them with a leader and, of course, direct them along the road that leads to our goal.

In order that the hand of the blind mob may not free itself from our guiding hand, we must every now and then enter into close communion with it, if not actually in person, at any rate through some of the most trusty of our brethren. When we are acknowledged as the only authority we shall discuss with the people personally on the market places, and we shall instruct them on questions of the political in such wise as may turn them in the direction that suits us.

Who is going to verify what is taught in the village schools? But what an envoy of the government or a king on his throne himself may say cannot but become immediately known to the whole State, for it will be spread abroad by the voice of the people.

In order not to annihilate the institutions of the goyim before it is time we have touched them with craft and delicacy, and have taken hold of the ends of the springs which move their mechanism. These springs lay in a strict but just sense of order; we have replaced them by the chaotic license of liberalism. We have got our hands into the administration of the law into the conduct of elections, into the press into liberty of the person, BUT PRINCIPALLY INTO EDUCATION AND TRAINING AS BEING THE CORNER-STONES OF A FREE EXISTENCE.

WE HAVE FOOLED, BEMUSED, AND CORRUPTED THE YOUTH OF THE GOYIM BY REARING THEM IN PRINCIPLES AND THEORIES WHICH ARE KNOWN TO US TO BE FALSE ALTHOUGH IT IS BY US THAT THEY HAVE BEEN INCULCATED.

Above the existing laws without substantially altering them, and by merely twisting them into contradictions of interpretations, we have erected something grandiose in the way of results. These results found expression first in the fact that the INTERPRETATIONS MASKED THE LAWS: afterwards they entirely hid them from the eyes of the governments owing to the impossibility of making anything out of the tangled web of legislation.

This is the origin of the theory of course of arbitration.

You may say the goyim will rise upon us, arms in hand if they guess what is going on before the time comes; but in the West we have against this a maneuver of such appalling terror that the very stoutest hearts quail - the undergrounds, metropolitans, those subterranean corridors which, before the time comes, will be driven under all the capitals and from whence those capitals will be blown into the air with all their organizations and archives.

Protocol 10

THE OUTSIDE APPEARANCES IN THE POLITICAL. THE
"GENIUS" OF RASCALITY. WHAT IS PROMISED BY A MASONIC
"COUP D'ETAT"? UNIVERSAL SUFFRAGE. SELF-IMPORTANCE.
LEADERS OF MASONRY. INSTITUTIONS AND THEIR
FUNCTIONS. THE POISON OF LIBERALISM. CONSTITUTION -
A SCHOOL OF PARTY DISCORDS. ERA OF REPUBLICS.
PRESIDENTS - THE PUPPETS OF MASONRY. RESPONSIBILITY
OF PRESIDENTS. "PANAMA" PART PLAYED BY CHAMBER OF
DEPUTIES AND PRESIDENT. MASONRY - THE LEGISLATIVE
FORCE. NEW REPUBLICAN CONSTITUTION. TRANSITION TO
FREEMASONIC "DESPOTISM." MOMENT FOR THE PROCLAMATION
OF "THE LORD OF ALL THE WORLD." INOCULATION OF
DISEASES AND OTHER WILES OF MASONRY.

Today I begin with repetition of what I said before, and I BEG YOU TO BEAR IN MIND THAT GOVERNMENTS AND PEOPLES ARE CONTENT IN THE POLITICAL WITH OUTSIDE APPEARANCES. And how, indeed, are the goyim to perceive the underlying meaning of things when their representatives give the best of their energies to enjoying themselves? For our policy it is of the greatest importance to take cognisance of this detail; it will be of assistance to us when we come to consider the division of authority, freedom of speech, of the press, of religion (faith), of the law of association, of equality before the law, of the inviolability of property, of the dwelling, of taxation (the idea of concealed taxes), of the reflex force of the laws. All these questions are such as ought not to be touched upon directly and openly before the people. In cases where it is indispensable to touch upon them they must not be categorically named, it must merely be declared without detailed exposition that the principles of contemporary law are acknowledged by us. The reason of keeping silence in this respect is that by not naming a principle we leave ourselves freedom of action, to drop this or that out of it without attracting notice; if they were all categorically named they would all appear to have been already given.

The mob cherishes a special affection and respect for the geniuses of political power and accepts all their deeds of violence with the admiring response: "rascally, well, yes, it is rascally, but it's clever! . . . a trick, if you like, but how craftily played, how magnificently done, what impudent audacity!" . . .

We count upon attracting all nations to the task of erecting the new fundamental structure, the project for which has been drawn up by us. This is why, before everything, it is indispensable for us to arm ourselves and to store up in ourselves that absolutely reckless audacity and irresistible might of the spirit which in the person of our active workers will break down all hindrances on our way.

WHEN WE HAVE ACCOMPLISHED OUR COUP D'ETAT WE SHALL SAY THEN TO THE VARIOUS PEOPLES: EVERYTHING HAS GONE TERRIBLY BADLY, ALL HAVE BEEN WORN OUT WITH SUFFERINGS. WE ARE DESTROYING THE CAUSES OF YOUR TORMENT - NATIONALITIES, FRONTIERS, DIFFERENCES OF COINAGES. YOU ARE AT LIBERTY, OF COURSE, TO PRONOUNCE SENTENCE UPON US, BUT CAN IT POSSIBLY BE A JUST ONE IF IT IS CONFIRMED BY YOU BEFORE YOU MAKE ANY TRIAL OF WHAT WE ARE OFFERING YOU." . . . THEN WILL THE MOB EXALT US AND BEAR US UP IN THEIR HANDS IN A UNANIMOUS TRIUMPH OF HOPES AND EXPECTATIONS. VOTING, WHICH WE HAVE MADE THE INSTRUMENT WHICH WILL SET US ON THE THRONE OF THE WORLD BY TEACHING EVEN THE VERY SMALLEST UNITS OF MEMBERS OF THE HUMAN RACE TO VOTE BY MEANS OF MEETINGS AND AGREEMENTS BY GROUPS, WILL THEN HAVE SERVED ITS PURPOSES AND WILL PLAY ITS PART THEN FOR THE LAST TIME BY A UNANIMITY OF DESIRE TO MAKE CLOSE ACQUAINTANCE WITH US BEFORE CONDEMNING US.

TO SECURE THIS WE MUST HAVE EVERYBODY VOTE WITHOUT DISTINCTION OF CLASSES AND QUALIFICATIONS, in order to establish an absolute majority, which cannot be got from the educated propertied classes. In this way by inculcating in all a sense of self-importance, we shall destroy among the goyim the importance of the family and its educational value and remove the possibility of individual minds splitting off, for the mob, handled by us, will not let them come to the front nor even give them a hearing; it is accustomed to listen to us only who pay it for obedience and attention. In this way we shall create a blind, mighty force which will never be in a position to move in any direction without the guidance of our agents set at its head by us as leaders of the mob. The people will submit to this regime because it will know that upon these leaders will depend its earnings, gratifications and the receipt of all kinds of benefits.

A scheme of government should come ready made from one brain, because it will never be clinched firmly if it is allowed to be split into fractional parts in the minds of many. It is allowable, therefore, for us to have cognisance of the scheme of action but not to discuss it lest we disturb its artfulness, the interdependence of its component parts, the practical force of the secret meaning of each clause. To discuss an make alterations in a labor of this kind by means of numerous votings is to impress upon it the stamp of all ratiocinations and misunderstandings which have failed to penetrate the depth and nexus of its plottings. We want our schemes to be forcible and suitably concocted. Therefore WE OUGHT NOT TO FLING THE WORK OF GENIUS OF OUR GUIDE to the fangs of the mob or even of a select company.

These schemes will not turn existing institutions upside down just yet. They will only affect changes in their economy and consequently in the whole combined movement of their progress, which will thus be directed along the paths laid down in our schemes.

Under various names there exists in all countries approximately one and the same thing. Representation, Ministry, Senate, State Council, Legislative and Executive Corps. I need not explain to you the mechanism of the relation of these institutions to one another, because you are aware of all that; only take note of the fact that each of the above-named institutions corresponds to some important function of the State, and I would beg you to remark that the word "important" I apply not to the institution but to the function, consequently it is not the institutions which are important but their functions. These institutions have divided up among themselves all the functions of government - administrative, legislative, executive, wherefore they have come to operate as do the organs in the human body. If we injure one part in the machinery of State, the State falls sick, like a human body, and will die.

When we introduced into the State organism the poison of Liberalism its whole political complexion underwent a change. States have been seized with a mortal illness-blood-poisoning. All that remains is to await the end of their death agony.

Liberalism produced Constitutional States, which took the place of what was the only safeguard of the goyim, namely, Despotism; and a CONSTITUTION, AS YOU WELL KNOW, IS NOTHING ELSE BUT A SCHOOL OF DISCORDS, misunderstandings, quarrels, disagreements, fruitless party agitations, party whims - in a word, a school of everything that serves to destroy the personality of State activity. THE TRIBUNE OF THE "TALKERIES" HAS, NO LESS EFFECTIVELY THAN THE PRESS, CONDEMNED THE RULERS TO INACTIVITY AND IMPOTENCE, and thereby rendered them useless and superfluous, for which reason indeed they have been in many countries deposed. THEN IT WAS THAT THE ERA OF REPUBLICS BECAME POSSIBLE OF REALISATION; AND THEN IT WAS THAT WE REPLACED THE RULER BY A CARICATURE OF A GOVERNMENT - BY A PRESIDENT, TAKEN FROM THE MOB, FROM THE MIDST OF OUR PUPPET CREATURES, OUR SLAVES. This was the foundation of the mine which we have laid under the goy people, I should rather say, under the goy peoples.

In the near future we shall establish the responsibility of presidents.

By that time we shall be in a position to disregard forms in carrying through matters for which our personal puppet will be responsible. What do we care if the ranks of those striving for power should be thinned, if there should arise a deadlock from the impossibility of finding presidents, a deadlock which will finally disorganize the country?

In order that our scheme may produce this result we shall arrange elections in favor of such presidents as have in their past some dark, undiscovered stain, some "Panama" or other - then they will be trustworthy agents for the accomplishment of our plans out of fear of revelations and from the natural desire of everyone who has attained power, namely, the retention of privileges, advantages and honor connected with the office of president. The chamber of deputies will provide cover for, will protect, will elect the president, but we shall take from it the right to propose new, or make changes in existing laws, for this right will be given by us to the responsible president, a puppet in our hands. Naturally, the authority of the president will then become a target for every possible form of attack, but we shall provide him with a means of self-defense in the right of an appeal to the people, for the decision of the people over the heads of their representatives, that is to say, an appeal to that same blind slave of ours - the majority of the mob. Independently of this we shall invest the president with the right of declaring a state of war. We shall justify this last right on the ground that the president as chief of the whole army of the country must have it at his disposal, in case of need for the defense of the new republican constitution, the right to defend which will belong to him as the responsible representative of this constitution.

It is easy to understand that in these conditions the key of the shrine will lie in our hands, and no one outside of ourselves will any longer direct the force of legislation.

Besides this we shall, with the introduction of the new republican constitution, take from the Chamber the right of interpellation on government measures, on the pretext of preserving political secrecy, and, further, we shall by the new constitution reduce the number of representatives to a minimum, thereby proportionately reducing political passions and the passion for politics. If, however, they should, which is hardly to be expected, burst into flame, even in this minimum, we shall nullify them by a stirring appeal and a reference to the majority of the whole people.... Upon the president will depend the appointment of presidents and vice-presidents of the Chamber and the Senate. Instead of constant sessions of Parliament we shall reduce their sittings to a few months. Moreover, the president, as chief of the executive power, will have the right to summon and dissolve Parliament, and, in the latter case, to prolong the time for the appointment of a new parliamentary assembly. But in order that the consequences of all these acts which in substance are illegal, should not, prematurely for our plans, fall upon the responsibility established by us of the president, WE SHALL INSTIGATE MINISTERS AND OTHER OFFICIALS OF THE HIGHER ADMINISTRATION ABOUT THE PRESIDENT TO EVADE HIS DISPOSITIONS BY TAKING MEASURES OF THEIR OWN, for doing which they will be made the scapegoats in his place.... This part we especially recommend to be given to be played by the Senate, the Council of State, or the Council of Ministers, but not to an individual official The president will, at our discretion, interpret the sense of such of the existing laws as admit of various interpretation; he will further annul them when we indicate to him the necessity to do so, besides this, he will have the right to propose temporary laws, and even new departures in the government constitutional working, the pretext both for the one and other being the requirements for the supreme welfare of the State.

By such measures we shall obtain the power of destroying little by little, step by step, all that at the outset when we enter on our rights, we are compelled to introduce into the constitutions of States to prepare for the transition to an imperceptible abolition of every kind of constitution, and then the time is come to turn every form of government into OUR DESPOTISM.

The recognition of our despot may also come before the destruction of the constitution; the moment for this recognition will come when the peoples, utterly wearied by the irregularities and incompetence - a matter which we shall arrange for - of their rulers, will clamor: " Away with them and give us one king over all the earth who will unite us and annihilate the causes of discords - frontiers, nationalities, religions, State debts - who will give us peace and quiet, which we cannot find under our rulers and representatives."

But you yourselves perfectly well know that TO PRODUCE THE POSSIBILITY OF THE EXPRESSION OF SUCH WISHES BY ALL THE NATIONS IT IS INDISSPENSABLE TO TROUBLE IN ALL

COUNTRIES THE PEOPLE'S RELATIONS WITH THEIR GOVERNMENTS SO AS TO UTTERLY EXHAUST HUMANITY WITH DISSENSION, HATRED, STRUGGLE, ENVY AND EVEN BY THE USE OF TORTURE, BY STARVATION, BY THE *INOCULATION OF DISEASES*, BY WANT, SO THAT THE GOYIM SEE NO OTHER ISSUE THAN TO TAKE REFUGE IN OUR COMPLETE SOVEREIGNTY IN MONEY AND IN ALL ELSE.

But if we give the nations of the world a breathing space the moment we long for is hardly likely ever to arrive.

PROTOCOL 11

PROGRAM OF THE NEW CONSTITUTION. CERTAIN DETAILS OF
THE PROPOSED REVOLUTION. THE GOYIM - A PACK OF
SHEEP. SECRET MASONRY AND ITS "SHOW" LODGES.

The State Council has been, as it were, the emphatic expression of the authority of the ruler: it will be, as the "show" part of the Legislative Corps, what may be called the editorial committee of the laws and decrees of the ruler.

This, then, is the program of the new constitution. We shall make Law, Right and Justice (1) in the guise of proposals to the Legislative Corps, (2) by decrees of the president under the guise of general regulations, of orders of the Senate and of resolutions of the State Council in the guise of ministerial orders, (3) and in case a suitable occasion should arise-in the form of a revolution in the State.

Having established approximately the "modus agendi" we will occupy ourselves with details of those combinations by which we have still to complete the revolution in the course of the machinery of State in the direction already indicated. By these combinations I mean the freedom of the Press, the right of association, freedom of conscience, the voting principle and many another that must disappear for ever from the memory of man or undergo a radical alteration the day after the promulgation of the new constitution. It is only at that moment that we shall be able at once to announce all our orders for afterwards, every noticeable alteration will be dangerous for the following reasons: if this alteration be brought in with harsh severity and in a sense of severity and limitations, it may lead to a feeling of despair caused by fear of new alterations in the same direction; if, on the other hand, it be brought in a sense of further indulgences it will be said that we have recognized our own wrongdoing and this will destroy the prestige of the infallibility of our authority, or else it will be said that we have become alarmed and are compelled to show a yielding disposition for which we shall get no thanks because it will be supposed to be compulsory.... Both the one and the other are injurious to the prestige of the new constitution. What we want is that from the first moment of its promulgation, while the peoples of the world are still stunned by the accomplished fact of the revolution, still in a condition of terror and uncertainty, they should recognize once for all that we are so strong, so inexpugnable, so superabundantly filled with power that in no case shall we take any account of them, and so far from paying any attention to their opinions or wishes we are ready and able to crush with irresistible power all expression or manifestation thereof at every moment and in every place, that we have seized at once everything we wanted and shall in no case divide our power with them.... Then in fear and trembling they will close their eyes to everything, and be content to await what will be the end of it all.

The goyim are a flock of sheep, and we are their wolves. And you know what happens when the wolves get hold of the flock? . . .

There is another reason also why they will close their eyes: for we shall keep promising them to give back all the liberties we have taken away as soon as we have quelled the enemies of peace and tamed all parties....

It is not worth while to say anything about how long a time they will be kept waiting for this return of their liberties....

For what purpose then have we invented this whole policy and insinuated it into the minds of the goys without giving them any chance to examine its underlying meaning? For what, indeed, if not in order to obtain in a roundabout way what is for our scattered tribe unattainable by the direct road? It Is this which has served as the basis for our organization of secret masonry which is not known to, and aims which are not even so much as suspected by, these GOY cattle, attracted by us into the "show" army of Masonic lodges in order to throw dust in the eyes of their fellows.

God has granted to us, His Chosen People, the gift of the dispersion, and in this which appears in all eyes to be our weakness, has come forth all our strength, which has now brought us to the threshold of sovereignty over all the world. There now remains not much more for us to build up upon the foundation we have laid.

PROTOCOL 12

MASONIC INTERPRETATION OF THE WORD "FREEDOM." FUTURE
OF THE PRESS IN THE FREEMASONIC KINGDOM. CONTROL OF
THE PRESS. CORRESPONDENCE AGENCIES. WHAT IS PROGRESS
AS UNDERSTOOD BY MASONRY? MORE ABOUT THE PRESS.
MASONIC SOLIDARITY IN THE PRESS OF TODAY. THE
AROUSING OF "PUBLIC" DEMANDS IN THE PROVINCES.
INFALLIBILITY OF THE NEW REGIME.

The word "freedom," which can be interpreted in various ways, is defined by us as follows: Freedom is the right to do that which the law allows. This interpretation of the word will at the proper time be of service to us because all freedom will thus be in our hands, since the laws will abolish or create only that which is desirable for us according to the aforesaid program.

We shall deal with the press in the following way: What is the part played by the press to-day? It serves to excite and inflame those passions which are needed for our purpose or else it serves selfish ends of parties. It is often vapid, unjust, mendacious, and the majority of the public have not the slightest idea what ends the press really serves. We shall saddle and bridle it with a tight curb: we shall do the same also with all productions of the printing press, for where would be the sense of getting rid of the attacks of the press if we remain targets for pamphlets and books? The produce of publicity, which nowadays is a source of heavy expense owing to the necessity of censoring it, will be turned by us into a very lucrative source of income to our State: we shall lay on it a special stamp tax and require deposits of caution-money before permitting the establishment of any organ of the press or of printing offices; these will then have to guarantee our government against any kind of attack on the part of the press. For any attempt to attack us, if such still be possible, we shall inflict fines without mercy. Such measures as stamp tax, deposit of caution-money and fines secured by these deposits, will bring in a huge income to the government. It is true that party organs might not spare money for the sake of publicity, but these we shall shut up at the second attack upon us. No one shall with impunity lay a finger on the aureole of our government infallibility. The pretext for stopping any publication will be the alleged plea that it is agitating the public mind without occasion or justification. I BEG YOU TO NOTE THAT AMONG THOSE MAKING ATTACKS UPON US WILL ALSO BE ORGANS ESTABLISHED BY US, BUT THEY WILL ATTACK EXCLUSIVELY POINTS THAT WE HAVE PRE-DETERMINED TO ALTER.

NOT A SINGLE ANNOUNCEMENT WILL REACH THE PUBLIC WITHOUT OUR CONTROL. Even now this is already being attained by us inasmuch as all news items are received by a few agencies, in whose offices they are focused from all parts of the world. These agencies will then be already entirely ours and will give publicity only to what we dictate to them.

If already now we have contrived to possess ourselves of the minds of the goy communities to such an extent that they all come near looking upon the events of the world through the colored glasses of those spectacles we are setting astride their noses: if already now there is not a single State where there exist for us any barriers to admittance into what goy stupidity calls State secrets: what will our position be then, when we shall be acknowledged supreme lords of the world in the person of our king of all the world....

Let us turn again to the FUTURE OF THE PRINTING PRESS. Every one desirous of being a publisher, librarian, or printer, will be obliged to provide himself with the diploma instituted therefor, which, in case of any fault, will be immediately impounded. With such measures THE INSTRUMENT OF THOUGHT WILL BECOME AN EDUCATIVE MEANS IN THE HANDS OF OUR GOVERNMENT, WHICH WILL NO LONGER ALLOW THE MASS OF THE NATION TO BE LED ASTRAY IN BY-WAYS AND FANTASIES ABOUT THE BLESSINGS OF PROGRESS. Is there any one of us who does not know that these phantom blessings are the direct roads to foolish imaginings which give birth to anarchical relations of men among themselves and towards authority, because progress, or rather the idea of progress, has introduced the conception of every kind of emancipation, but has failed to establish its limits.... All the so-called liberals are anarchists, if not in fact, at any rate in thought. Every one of them is hunting after phantoms of freedom, and falling exclusively into license, that is, into the anarchy of protest for the sake of protest....

We turn to the periodical press. We shall impose on it, as on all printed matter, stamp taxes per sheet and deposits of caution-money, and books of less than 30 sheets will pay double. We shall reckon them as pamphlets in order, on the one hand, to reduce the number of magazines, which are the worst form of printed poison, and, on the other, in order that this measure may force writers into such lengthy productions that they will be little read, especially as they will be costly. At the same time what we shall publish ourselves to influence mental development in the direction laid down for our profit will be cheap and will be read voraciously. The tax will bring vapid literary ambitions within bounds and the liability to penalties will make literary men dependent upon us. And if there should be any found who are desirous of writing against us, they will not find any person eager to print their productions. Before accepting any production for publication in print the publisher or printer will have to apply to the authorities for permission to do so. Thus we shall know beforehand of all tricks preparing against us and shall nullify them by getting ahead with explanations on the subject treated of.

Literature and journalism are two of the most important educative forces, and therefore our government will become proprietor of the majority of the journals. This will neutralize the injurious influence of the privately owned press and will put us in possession of a tremendous influence upon the public mind... If we give permits for ten journals, we shall ourselves found thirty, and so on in the same proportion. This, however, must in nowise be suspected by the public. For which reason all journals published by us will be of the most opposite, in appearance, tendencies and opinions, thereby creating confidence in us and bringing over to us our quite unsuspicious opponents, who will thus fall into our trap and be rendered harmless.

In the front rank will stand organs of an official character. They will always stand guard over our interests, and therefore their influence will be comparatively insignificant.

In the second rank will be the semi-official organs, whose part it will be to attract the tepid and indifferent.

In the third rank we shall set up our own, to all appearance, opposition, which, in at least one of its organs will present what looks like the very antipodes to us. Our real opponents at heart will accept this simulated opposition as their own and will show us their cards.

All our newspapers will be of all possible complexions - aristocratic, republican, revolutionary, even anarchical - for so long, of course, as the constitution exists.... Like the Indian idol Vishnu they will have a hundred hands and every one of them will have a finger on any one of the public opinions as required. When a pulse quickens these hands will lead opinion in the direction of our aims, for an excited patient loses all power of judgment and easily yields to suggestion. Those fools who will think they are repeating the opinion of a newspaper of their own camp will be repeating our opinion or any opinion that seems desirable for us. In the vain belief that they are following the organ of their party they will in fact follow the flag which we hang out for them.

In order to direct our newspaper militia in this sense we must take especial and minute care in organizing this matter. Under the title of central department of the press we shall institute literary gatherings at which our agents will without attracting attention issue the orders and watchwords of the day. By discussing and controverting, but always superficially without touching the essence of the matter, our organs will carry on a sham fight fusillade with the official newspapers solely for the purpose of giving occasion for us to express ourselves more fully than could well be done from the outset in official announcements, whenever, of course, that is to our advantage.

THESE ATTACKS UPON US WILL ALSO SERVE ANOTHER PURPOSE, NAMELY, THAT OUR SUBJECTS WILL BE CONVINCED OF THE EXISTENCE OF FULL FREEDOM OF SPEECH AND SO GIVE OUR AGENTS AN OCCASION TO AFFIRM THAT ALL ORGANS WHICH OPPOSE US ARE EMPTY

BABBLERS, since they are incapable of finding any substantial objections to our orders.

Methods of organization like these, imperceptible to the public eye but absolutely true, are the best calculated to succeed in bringing the attention and the confidence of the public to the side of our government. Thanks to such methods we shall be in a position as from time to time may be required, to excite or to tranquillize the public mind on political questions, to persuade or to confuse, printing now truth, now lies, facts or their contradictions, according as they may be well or ill received, always very cautiously feeling our ground before stepping upon it.... WE SHALL HAVE A SURE TRIUMPH OVER OUR OPPONENTS SINCE THEY WILL NOT HAVE AT THEIR DISPOSITION ORGANS OF THE PRESS IN WHICH THEY CAN GIVE FULL AND FINAL EXPRESSION TO THEIR VIEWS owing to the aforesaid methods of dealing with the press. We shall not even need to refute them except very superficially.

Trial shots like these, fired by us in the third rank of our press, in case of need, will be energetically refuted by us in our semi-official organs.

Even nowadays, already, to take only the French press, there are forms which reveal freemasonic solidarity in acting on the watchword: all organs of the press are bound together by professional secrecy; like the augurs of old, not one of their numbers will give away the secret of his sources of information unless it be resolved to make announcement to them. Not one journalist will venture to betray this secret, for not one of them is ever admitted to practice literature unless his whole past has some disgraceful sore or other. . . These sores would be immediately revealed. So long as they remain the secret of a few the prestige of the journalist attracts the majority of the country - the mob follows after him with enthusiasm.

Our calculations are especially extended to the provinces. It is indispensable for us to inflame there those hopes and impulses with which we could at any moment fall upon the capital, and we shall represent to the capitals that these expressions are the independent hopes and impulses of the provinces. Naturally, the source of them will be always one and the same - ours. WHAT WE NEED IS THAT, UNTIL SUCH

TIME AS WE ARE IN THE PLENITUDE OF POWER, THE CAPITALS SHOULD FIND THEMSELVES STIFLED BY THE PROVINCIAL OPINION OF THE NATION, i.e., OF A MAJORITY ARRANGED BY OUR AGENTUR. What we need is that at the psychological moment the capitals should not be in a position to discuss an accomplished fact for the simple reason, if for no other, that it has been accepted by the public opinion of a majority in the provinces.

WHEN WE ARE IN THE PERIOD OF THE NEW REGIME TRANSITIONAL TO THAT OF OUR ASSUMPTION OF FULL SOVEREIGNTY. WE MUST NOT ADMIT ANY REVELATIONS BY THE PRESS OF ANY FORM OF PUBLIC DISHONESTY; IT IS NECESSARY THAT THE NEW REGIME SHOULD BE THOUGHT TO HAVE SO PERFECTLY CONTENTED EVERYBODY THAT EVEN CRIMINALITY HAS DISAPPEARED... Cases of the manifestation of criminality should remain known only to their victims and to chance witnesses - no more.

PROTOCOL 13

THE NEED FOR DAILY BREAD. QUESTIONS OF THE
POLITICAL. QUESTIONS OF INDUSTRY. AMUSEMENTS.
PEOPLE'S PALACES. "TRUTH IS ONE." THE GREAT
PROBLEMS.

The need for daily bread forces the goyim to keep silence and be our humble servants. Agents taken on to our press from among the goyim will at our order discuss anything which it is inconvenient for us to issue directly in official documents, and we meanwhile, quietly amid the din of the discussion so raised, shall simply take and carry through such measures as we wish and then offer them to the public as an accomplished fact. No one will dare to demand the abrogation of a matter once settled, all the more so as it will be represented as an improvement.... And immediately the press will distract the current of thought towards new questions (have we not trained people always to be seeking something new?). Into the discussions of these new questions will throw themselves those of the brainless dispensers of fortunes who are not able even now to understand that they have not the remotest conception about the matters which they undertake to discuss. Questions of the political are unattainable for any save those who have guided it already for many ages, the creators.

From all this you will see that in securing the opinion of the mob we are only facilitating the working of our machinery, and you may remark that it is not for actions but for words issued by us on this or that question that we seem to seek approval. We are constantly making public declaration that we are guided in all our undertakings by the hope, joined to the conviction, that are we serving the common weal.

In order to distract people who may be too troublesome from discussions of questions of the political we are now putting forward what we allege to be new questions of the political, namely, questions of industry. In this sphere let them discuss themselves silly! The masses are agreed to remain inactive, to take a rest from what they suppose to be political activity (which we trained them to in order to use them as a means of combating the goy governments) only on condition of being found new employments, in which we are prescribing them something that looks like the same political object. In order that the masses themselves may not guess what they are about WE FURTHER DISTRACT THEM WITH AMUSEMENTS, GAMES, PASTIMES, PASSIONS, PEOPLE'S PALACES... SOON WE SHALL BEGIN THROUGH THE PRESS TO PROPOSE COMPETITIONS IN ART, IN SPORT OF ALL KINDS: these interests will finally distract their minds from questions in which we should find ourselves compelled to oppose them. Growing more and more disaccustomed to reflect and form any opinions of their own, people will begin to talk in the same tone as we, because we alone shall be offering them new directions for thought . . . of course through such persons as will not be suspected of solidarity with us.

The part played by the liberals, utopian dreamers, will be finally played out when our government is acknowledged. Till such time they will continue to do us good service. Therefore we shall continue to direct their minds to all sorts of vain conceptions of fantastic theories, new and apparently progressive: for have we not with complete success turned the brainless heads of the goyim with progress till there is not among the goyim one mind able to perceive that under this word lies a departure from truth in all cases where it is not a question of material inventions, for truth is one and in it there is no place for progress. Progress, like a fallacious idea serves to obscure truth so that none may know it except us the Chosen of God, its guardians.

When we come into our kingdom our orators will expound great problems which have turned humanity upside down in order to bring it at the end under our beneficent rule.

Who will ever suspect then that ALL THESE PEOPLE WERE STAGE-MANAGED BY US ACCORDING TO A POLITICAL PLAN WHICH NO ONE HAS SO MUCH AS GUESSED AT IN THE COURSE OF MANY CENTURIES? . . .

PROTOCOL 14

THE RELIGION OF THE FUTURE. FUTURE CONDITIONS OF SERFDOM. INACCESSIBILITY OF KNOWLEDGE REGARDING THE RELIGION OF THE FUTURE. PORNOGRAPHY AND THE PRINTED MATTER OF THE FUTURE.

When we come into our kingdom it will be undesirable for us that there should exist any other religion than ours of the One God with whom our destiny is bound up by our position as the Chosen People and through whom our same destiny is united with the destinies of the world. We must therefore sweep away all other forms of belief. If this gives birth to the atheist whom we see to-day, it will not, being only a transitional stage, interfere with our views, but will serve as a warning for those generations which will hearken to our preaching of the religion of Moses, that, by its stable and thoroughly elaborated system has brought all the peoples of the world into subjection to us. Therein we shall emphasize its mystical right, on which as we shall say, all its educative power is based.... Then at every possible opportunity we shall publish articles in which we shall make comparisons between our beneficent rule and those of past ages. The blessings of tranquility though it be a tranquility forcibly brought about by centuries of agitation will throw into higher relief the benefits to which we shall point. The errors of the goyim government will be depicted by us in the most vivid hues. We shall implant such an abhorrence of them that the peoples will prefer tranquility in a state of serfdom to those rights of vaunted freedom which have tortured humanity and exhausted the very sources of human existence, sources which have been exploited by a mob of rascally adventurers who know not what they do.... USELESS CHANGES OF FORMS OF GOVERNMENT TO WHICH WE INSTIGATED THE GOYIM WHEN WE WERE UNDERMINING THEIR STATE STRUCTURES, WILL HAVE SO WEARIED THE PEOPLES BY

THAT TIME THAT THEY WILL PREFER TO SUFFER ANYTHING UNDER US RATHER THAN RUN THE RISK OF ENDURING AGAIN ALL THE AGITATIONS AND MISERIES THEY HAVE GONE THROUGH.

At the same time we shall not omit to emphasize the historical mistakes of the goy governments which have tormented humanity for so many centuries by their lack of understanding of everything that constitutes the true good of humanity in their chase after fantastic schemes of social blessings and have never noticed that these schemes kept on producing a worse and never a better state of the universal relations which are the basis of human life....

The whole force of our principles and methods will lie in the fact that we shall present them and expound them as a splendid contrast to the dead and decomposed old order of things in social life.

Our philosophers will discuss all the shortcomings of the various beliefs of the GOYIM, BUT NO ONE WILL EVER BRING UNDER DISCUSSION OUR FAITH FROM ITS TRUE POINT OF VIEW SINCE THIS WILL BE FULLY LEARNED BY NONE SAVE OURS, WHO WILL NEVER DARE TO BETRAY ITS SECRETS.

IN COUNTRIES KNOWN AS PROGRESSIVE AND ENLIGHTENED WE HAVE CREATED A SENSELESS, FILTHY, ABOMINABLE LITERATURE. For some time after our entrance to power we shall continue to encourage its existence in order to provide a telling relief by contrast to the speeches, party program, which will be distributed from exalted quarters of ours.... Our wise men, trained to become leaders of the goyim, will compose speeches, projects, memoirs, articles, which will be used by us to influence the minds of the goyim, directing them towards such understanding and forms of knowledge as have been determined by us.

PROTOCOL 15

One-day "coup d'état (revolution) over all the world. Executions. Future lot of GOYIM-masons. Mysticism of authority. Multiplication of freemasonic lodges. Central governing board of freemasonic elders. The "Azev-tactics." Masonry as leader and guide of all secret societies. Significance of public applause. Collectivism. Victims. Executions of masons. Fall of the prestige of laws and authority. Our position as the Chosen people. Brevity and clarity of the laws of the kingdom of the future. Obedience to orders. Measures against abuse of authority. Severity of penalties. Age-limit for judges. Liberalism of judges and authorities. The money of all the world. Absolutism of masonry. Right of appeal. Patriarchal "outside appearance" of the power of the future "ruler." Apotheosis of the ruler. The right of the strong as one and only right. The King of Israel. Patriarch of all the world.

When we at last definitely come into our kingdom by the aid of COUPS D'ETAT prepared everywhere for one and the same day, after the worthlessness of all existing forms of government has been definitely acknowledged (and not a little time will pass before that comes about, perhaps even a whole century) we shall make it our task to see that against us such things as plots shall no longer exist. With this purpose we shall slay without mercy all who take arms (in hand) to oppose our coming into our kingdom. Every kind of new institution of anything like a secret society will also be punished with death; those of them which are now in existence are known to us, serve us and have served us, we shall disband and send into exile to continents far removed from Europe. IN THIS WAY WE SHALL PROCEED WITH THOSE GOY-MASONS WHO

KNOW TOO MUCH; such of these as we may for some reason spare will be kept in constant fear of exile. We shall promulgate a law making all former members of secret societies liable to exile from Europe as the centre of our rule.

Resolutions of our government will be final, without appeal.

In the goy societies in which we have planted and deeply rooted discord and protestantism, the only possible way of restoring order is to employ merciless measures that prove the direct force of authority: no regard must be paid to the victims who fall, they suffer for the well-being of the future. The attainment of that well-being, even at the expense of sacrifices, is the duty of any kind of government that acknowledges as justification for its existence not only its privileges but its obligations. The principal guarantee of stability of rule is to confirm the aureole of power and this aureole is attained only by such a majestic inflexibility of might as shall carry on its face the emblems of inviolability from mystical causes - from the choice of God. SUCH WAS, UNTIL RECENT TIMES, THE RUSSIAN AUTOCRACY, THE ONE AND ONLY SERIOUS FOE WE HAD IN THE WORLD, WITHOUT COUNTING THE PAPACY. Bear in mind the example when Italy, drenched with blood, never touched a hair of the head of Sulla who had poured forth that blood: Sulla enjoyed an apotheosis for his might in the eyes of the people, though they had been torn in pieces by him, but his intrepid return to Italy ringed him round with inviolability. The people do not lay a finger on him who hypnotizes them by his daring and strength of mind.

Meantime, however, until we come into our kingdom, we shall act in the contrary way: we shall create and multiply freemasonic lodges in all the countries of the world, absorb into them all who may become or who are prominent in public activity, for in these lodges we shall find our principal intelligence office and means of influence. All these lodges we shall bring under one central administration, known to us alone and to all others absolutely unknown, which will be composed of our learned elders. The lodges will have their representatives who will serve to screen the above-mentioned administration of masonry and from whom will issue the watchword and program. In these lodges we shall tie together the knot which binds together all revolutionary and liberal elements. Their competition will be made up of all strata of society. The most secret political plot will be known to us and will fall under our guiding hands on the very day of their conception. AMONG THE MEMBERS OF THESE LODGES WILL BE ALMOST ALL THE AGENTS OF INTERNATIONAL AND NATIONAL POLICE since their service is for us irreplaceable in the respect that the police is in a position not only to use its own particular measures with the insubordinate, but also to screen our activities and provide pretexts for discontents, ET CETERA.

The class of people who most willingly enter into secret societies are those who live by their wits, careerists, and in general people, mostly light-minded, with whom we shall have no difficulty in dealing and in using to wind up the mechanism of the machine devised by us. If this world grows agitated the meaning of that will be that we have had to stir it up in order to break up its too great solidarity. BUT IF THERE SHOULD ARISE IN ITS MIDST A PLOT, THEN AT THE HEAD OF THAT PLOT WILL BE NO OTHER THAN ONE OF OUR MOST TRUSTED SERVANTS. It is natural that we and no other should lead MASONIC activities, for we know whither we are leading, we know the final goal of every form of activity whereas the goyim have knowledge of nothing, not even of the immediate effect of action; they put before themselves, usually, the momentary reckoning of the satisfaction of their self-opinion in the accomplishment of their thought without even remarking that the very conception never belonged to their initiative but to our instigation of their thought....

The goyim enter the lodges out of curiosity or in the hope by their means to get a nibble at the public pie, and some
of them in order to obtain a hearing before the public for their impracticable and groundless fantasies: they thirst for the emotion of success and applause, of which we are remarkably generous. And the reason why we give them this success is to make use of the high conceit of themselves to which it gives birth, for that insensibly disposes them to assimilate our suggestions without being on their guard against them in the fullness of their confidence that it is their own infallibility which is giving utterance to their own thoughts and that it is impossible for them to borrow those of others....You cannot imagine to what extent the wisest of the

goyim can be brought to a state of unconscious naivete in the presence of this condition of high conceit of themselves, and at the same time how easy it is to take the heart out of them by the slightest ill success, though it be nothing more than the stoppage of the applause they had, and to reduce them to a slavish submission for the sake of winning a renewal of success.... BY SO MUCH AS OURS DISREGARD SUCCESS IF ONLY THEY CAN CARRY THROUGH THEIR PLANS, BY SO MUCH THE GOYIM ARE WILLING TO SACRIFICE ANY PLANS ONLY TO HAVE SUCCESS. This psychology of theirs materially facilitates for us the task of setting them in the required direction. These tigers in appearance have the souls of sheep and the wind blows freely through their heads. We have set them on the hobby-horse of an idea about the absorption of individuality by the symbolic unit of COLLECTIVISM.... They have never yet and they never will have the sense to reflect that this hobby-horse is a manifest violation of the most important law of nature which has established from the very creation of the world one unit unlike another and precisely for the purpose of instituting individuality....

If we have been able to bring them to such a pitch of stupid blindness is it not a proof, and an amazingly clear proof, of the degree to which the mind of the goyim is undeveloped in comparison with our mind? This it is, mainly, which guarantees our success.

And how far-seeing were our learned elders in ancient times when they said that to attain a serious end it behoves not to stop at any means or to count the victims sacrificed for the sake of that end.... We have not counted the victims of the seed of the goy cattle, though we have sacrificed many of our own, but for that we have now already given them such a position on the earth as they could not even have dreamed of. The comparatively small numbers of the victims from the number of ours have preserved our nationality from destruction.

Death is the inevitable end for all. It is better to bring that end nearer to those who hinder our affairs than to ourselves, to the founders of this affair. WE EXECUTE MASONS IN SUCH WISE THAT NONE SAVE THE BROTHERHOOD CAN EVER HAVE A SUSPICION OF IT, NOT EVEN THE VICTIMS THEMSELVES OF OUR DEATH

SENTENCE, THEY ALL DIE WHEN REQUIRED AS IF FROM A NORMAL KIND OF ILLNESS... Knowing this, even the brotherhood in its turn dare not protest. By such methods we have plucked out of the midst of MASONRY the very root of protest against our disposition. While preaching liberalism to the goyim we at the same time keep our own people and our agents in a state of unquestioning submission.

Under our influence the execution of the laws of the goyim has been reduced to a minimum. The prestige of the law has been exploded by the liberal interpretations introduced into this sphere. In the most important and fundamental affairs and questions judges decide as we dictate to them, see matters in the light wherewith we enfold them for the administration of the goyim, of course, through persons who are our tools though we do not appear to have anything in common with them - by newspaper opinion or by other means.... Even senators and the higher administration accept our counsels. The purely brute mind of the goyim is incapable of use for analysis and observation, and still more for the foreseeing whither a certain manner of setting a question may tend.

In this difference in capacity for thought between the goyim and ourselves may be clearly discerned the seal of our position on the Chosen People and of our higher quality of humaness, in contradistinction to the brute mind of the goyim. Their eyes are open, but see nothing before them and do not invent (unless, perhaps, material things). From this it is plain that nature herself has destined us to guide and rule the world. When comes the time of our overt rule, the time to manifest its blessings, we shall remake all legislatures, all our laws will be brief, plain, stable, without any kind of interpretations, so that anyone will he in a position to know them perfectly. The main feature which will run right through them is submission to orders, and this principle will be carried to a grandiose height.

Every abuse will then disappear in consequence of the responsibility of all down to the lowest unit before the higher authority of the representative of power. Abuses of power subordinate to this last instance will be so mercilessly punished that none will be found anxious to try experiments with their own powers. We shall follow up jealously every action of the administration on which depends the smooth running of the machinery of the State, for slackness in this produces slackness everywhere; not a single case of illegality or abuse of power will be left without exemplary punishment.

Concealment of guilt, connivance between those in the service of the administration - all this kind of evil will disappear after the very first examples of severe punishment. The aureole of our power demands suitable, that is, cruel, punishments for the slightest infringement, for the sake of gain, of its supreme prestige. The sufferer, though his punishment may exceed his fault, will count as a soldier falling on the administrative field of battle in the interest of authority, principle and law, which do not permit that any of those who hold the reins of the public coach should turn aside from the public highway to their own private paths. FOR EXAMPLE: OUR JUDGES WILL KNOW THAT WHENEVER THEY FEEL DISPOSED TO PLUME THEMSELVES ON FOOLISH CLEMENCY THEY ARE VIOLATING THE LAW OF JUSTICE WHICH IS INSTITUTED FOR THE EXEMPLARY EDIFICATION OF MEN BY PENALTIES FOR LAPSES AND NOT FOR DISPLAY OF THE SPIRITUAL QUALITIES OF THE JUDGE.... Such qualities it is proper to show in private life, but not in a public square which is the educational basis of human life.

Our legal staff will serve not beyond the age of 55, firstly because old men more obstinately hold to prejudiced opinions, and are less capable of submitting to new directions and second because this will give us the possibility by this measure of securing elasticity in the changing of staff, which will thus the more easily bend under our pressure: he who wishes to keep his place will have to give blind obedience to deserve it. In general, our judges will be elected by us only from among those who thoroughly understand that the part they have to play is to punish and apply laws and not to dream about the manifestations of liberalism at the expense of the educationary scheme of the State as the goyim in these days imagine it to be.... This method of shuffling the staff will serve also to explode any collective solidarity of those in the same service and will bind all to the interests of the government upon which their fate will depend. The young generation of judges will be trained in certain views regarding the inadmissibility of any abuses that might disturb the established order of our subjects among themselves.

In these days the judges of the goyim create indulgences to every kind of crime, not having a just understanding of their office, because the rulers of the present age in appointing judges to office tale no care to inculcate in them a sense of duty and consciousness of the matter which is demanded of them. As a brute beast lets out its young in search of prey, so do the goyim give their subjects places of profit without thinking to make clear to them for what purpose such place was created. This is the reason why their governments are being ruined by their own forces through the acts of their own administration.

Let us borrow from the example of the results these actions yet another lesson for our government.

We shall root out liberalism from all the important strategic posts of our government on which depends the training of subordinates for our State structure. Such posts will fall exclusively to those who have been trained by us for administrative rule. To the possible objection that the retirement of old servants will cost the Treasury heavily, I reply, firstly, they will be provided with some private service in place of what they lose, and, secondly, I have to remark that all the money in the world will be concentrated in our hands, consequently it is not our government that has to fear expense. Our absolutism will in all things be logically consecutive and therefore in each one of its decrees our supreme will will be respected and unquestionably fulfilled: it will ignore all murmurs, all discontents of every kind and will destroy to the root every kind of manifestation of them in act by punishment of an exemplary character.

We shall abolish the right of cassation, which will be transferred exclusively to our disposal - to the cognisance of him who rules, for we must not allow the conception among the people of a thought that there could be such a thing

as a decision that is not right of judges set up by us. If, however, anything like this should occur, we shall ourselves cassate the decision, but inflict therewith such exemplary punishment on the judge for lack of understanding of his duty and the purpose of his appointment as will prevent a repetition of such cases.... I repeat that it must be borne in mind that we shall know every step of our administration which only needs to be closely watched for the people to be content with us, for it has the right to demand from a good government a good official.

OUR GOVERNMENT WILL HAVE THE APPEARANCE OF A PATRIARCHAL PATERNAL GUARDIANSHIP ON THE PART OF OUR RULER. Our own nation and our own subjects will discern in his person a father caring for their every need, their every act, their every inter-relation as subjects one with another, as well as their relations to the ruler. They will then be so thoroughly imbued with the thought that it is impossible for them to dispense with this wardship and guidance, if they wish to live in peace and quiet, THAT THEY WILL ACKNOWLEDGE THE AUTOCRACY OF OUR RULER WITH A DEVOTION BORDERING ON APOTHEOSIS, especially when they are convinced that those whom we set up do not put their own in place of his authority, but only blindly execute his dictates. They will be rejoiced that we have regulated everything in their lives as is done by wise parents who desire to train their children in the cause of duty and submission. For the peoples of the world in regard to the secrets of our polity are ever through the ages only children under age, precisely as are their governments.

As you see, I found our despotism on right and duty: the right to compel the execution of duty is the direct obligation of a government which is a father for its subjects. It has the right of the strong that it may use it for the benefit of directing humanity towards that order which is defined by nature, namely, submission. Everything in the world is in a state of submission, if not to man, then to circumstances or its own inner character, in all cases, to what is stronger. And so shall we be this something stronger for the sake of good.

We are obliged without hesitation to sacrifice individuals, who commit a breach of established order, for in the exemplary punishment of evil lies a great educational problem.

When the King of Israel sets upon his sacred head the crown offered him by Europe he will become patriarch of the world. The indispensable victims offered by him in consequence of their suitability will never reach the number of victims offered in the course of centuries by the mania of magnificence, the emulation between the goy governments.

Our King will be in constant communion with the peoples, making to them from the tribune speeches which fame will in that same hour distribute all over the world.

PROTOCOL 16

EMASCULATION OF THE UNIVERSITIES. SUBSTITUTE FOR CLASSICISM. TRAINING AND CALLING. ADVERTISEMENT OF THE AUTHORITY OF "THE RULER" IN THE SCHOOLS. ABOLITION OF FREEDOM OF INSTRUCTION. NEW THEORIES. INDEPENDENCE OF THOUGHT. TEACHING BY OBJECT LESSONS.

In order to effect the destruction of all collective forces except ours we shall emasculate the first stage of collectivism - the UNIVERSITIES, by re-educating them in a new direction. THEIR OFFICIALS AND PROFESSORS WILL BE PREPARED FOR THEIR BUSINESS BY DETAILED SECRET PROGRAMMES OF ACTION FROM WHICH THEY WILL NOT WITH IMMUNITY DIVERGE, NOT BY ONE IOTA. THEY WILL BE APPOINTED WITH ESPECIAL PRECAUTION, AND WILL BE SO PLACED AS TO BE WHOLLY DEPENDENT UPON THE GOVERNMENT.

We shall exclude from the course of instruction State Law as also all that concerns the political question. These subjects will be taught to a few dozens of persons chosen for their pre-eminent capacities from among the number of the initiated. THE UNIVERSITIES MUST NO LONGER SEND OUT FROM THEIR HALLS MILKSOPS CONCOCTING PLANS FOR A CONSTITUTION, LIKE A COMEDY OR A TRADEDY, BUSYING THEMSELVES WITH QUESTIONS OF POLICY IN WHICH EVEN THEIR OWN FATHERS NEVER HAD ANY POWER OF THOUGHT.

The ill-guided acquaintance of a large number of persons with questions of polity creates utopian dreamers and bad subjects, as you can see for yourselves from the example of the universal education in this direction of the goyim. We must introduce into their education all those principles which have so brilliantly broken up their order. But when we are in power we shall remove every kind of disturbing subject from the course of education and shall make out of the youth obedient children of authority, loving him who rules as the support and hope of peace and quiet.

Classicism, as also any form of study of ancient history, in which there are more bad than good examples, we shall replace with the study of the program of the future. We shall erase from the memory of men all facts of previous centuries which are undesirable to us, and leave only those which depict all the errors of the government of the goyim. The study of practical life, of the obligations of order, of the relations of people one to another, of avoiding bad and selfish examples, which spread the infection of evil, and similar questions of an educative nature, will stand in the forefront of the teaching program, which will be drawn up on a separate plan for each calling or state of life, in no wise generalizing the teaching. This treatment of the question has special importance.

Each state of life must be trained within strict limits corresponding to its destination and work in life. The OCCASIONAL GENIUS HAS ALWAYS MANAGED AND ALWAYS WILL MANAGE TO SLIP THROUGH INTO OTHER STATES OF LIFE, BUT IT IS THE MOST PERFECT FOLLY FOR THE SAKE OF THIS RARE OCCASIONAL GENIUS TO LET THROUGH INTO RANKS FOREIGN TO THEM THE UNTALENTED WHO THUS ROB OF THEIR PLACES THOSE WHO BELONG TO THOSE RANKS BY BIRTH OR EMPLOYMENT. YOU KNOW YOURSELVES IN WHAT ALL THIS HAS ENDED FOR THE GOYIM WHO ALLOWED THIS CRYING ABSURDITY.

In order that he who rules may be seated firmly in the hearts and minds of his subjects it is necessary for the time of his activity to instruct the whole nation in the schools and on the market places about his meaning and his acts and all his beneficent initiatives.

We shall abolish every kind of freedom of instruction. Learners of all ages will have the right to assemble together with their parents in the educational establishments as it were in a club: during these assemblies, on holidays, teachers will read what will pass as free lectures on questions of human relations, of the laws of examples, of the limitations which are born of unconscious relations, and, finally, of the philosophy of new theories not yet declared to the world. These theories will be raised by us to the stage of a dogma of faith as a transitional stage towards our faith. On the completion of this exposition of our program of action in the present and the future I will read you the principles of these theories.

In a word, knowing by the experience of many centuries that people live and are guided by ideas, that these ideas are imbibed by people only by the aid of education provided with equal success for all ages of growth, but of course by varying methods, we shall swallow up and confiscate to our own use the last scintilla of independence of thought, which we have for long past been directing towards subjects and ideas useful for us. The system of bridling thought is already at work in the so-called system of teaching by OBJECT LESSONS, the purpose of which is to turn the goyim into unthinking submissive brutes waiting for things to be presented before their eyes in order to form an idea of them.... In France, one of our best agents, Bourgeois, has already made public a new program of teaching by object lessons.

PROTOCOL 17

ADVOCACY. INFLUENCE OF THE PRIESTHOOD OF THE GOYIM. FREEDOM OF CONSCIENCE. PAPAL COURT. KING OF THE JEWS AS PATRIARCH-POPE. HOW TO FIGHT THE EXISTING CHURCH. FUNCTION OF CONTEMPORARY PRESS. ORGANIZATION OF POLICE. VOLUNTEER POLICE. ESPIONAGE ON THE PATTERN OF THE KABAL ESPIONAGE. ABUSES OF AUTHORITY.

The practice of advocacy produces men cold, cruel, persistent, unprincipled, who in all cases take up an impersonal, purely legal standpoint. They have the inveterate habit to refer everything to its value for the defense and not to the public welfare of its results. They do not usually decline to undertake any defense whatever, they strive for an acquittal at all costs, caviling over every petty crux of jurisprudence and thereby they demoralize justice. For this reason we shall set this profession into narrow frames which will keep it inside this sphere of executive public service. Advocates, equally with judges, will be deprived of the right of communication with litigants; they will receive business only from the court and will study it by notes of re- port and documents, defending their clients after they have been interrogated in court on facts that have appeared. They will receive an honorarium without regard to the quality of the defense. This will render them mere reporters on law-business in the interests of justice and as counterpoise to the proctor who will be the reporter in the interests of prosecution; this will shorten business before the courts. In this way will be established a practice of honest unprejudiced defense conducted not from personal interest but by conviction. This will also, by the way, remove the present practice of corrupt bargain between advocates to agree only to let that side win which pays most...

WE HAVE LONG PAST TAKEN CARE TO DISCREDIT THE

PRIESTHOOD OF THE GOYIM, and thereby to ruin their mission on earth which in these days might still be a great hindrance to us. Day by day its influence on the peoples of the world is falling lower. FREEDOM OF CONSCIENCE has been declared everywhere, SO THAT NOW ONLY YEARS DIVIDE US FROM THE MOMENT OF THE COMPLETE WRECKING OF THAT CHRISTIAN RELIGION: as to other religions we shall have still less difficulty in dealing with them, but it would be premature to speak of this now. We shall set clericalism and clericals into such narrow frames as to make their influence move in retrogressive proportion to its former progress.

When the time comes finally to destroy the papal court the finger of an invisible hand will point the nations towards this court. When, however, the nations fling themselves upon it, we shall come forward in the guise of its defenders as if to save excessive bloodshed. By this diversion we shall penetrate to its very bowels and be sure we shall never come out again until we have gnawed through the entire strength of this place.

THE KING OF THE JEWS WILL BE THE REAL POPE OF THE UNIVERSE, THE PATRIARCH OF AN INTERNATIONAL CHURCH.

But, IN THE MEANTIME, while we are re-educating youth in new traditional religions and afterwards in ours, WE SHALL NOT OVERTLY LAY A FINGER ON EXISTING CHURCHES, BUT WE SHALL FIGHT AGAINST THEM BY CRITICISM CALCULATED TO PRODUCE SCHISM...

In general, then, our contemporary press will continue to CONVICT State affairs, religions, incapacities of the goyim, always using the most unprincipled expressions in order by every means to lower their prestige in the manner which can only be practiced by the genius of our gifted tribe...

Our kingdom will be an apologia of the divinity Vishnu, in whom is found its personification - in our hundred hands will be, one in each, the springs of the machinery of social life. We shall see every- thing without the aid of official police which, in that scope of its rights which we elaborated for the use of the goyim, hinders governments from seeing. In our program ONE - THIRD OF OUR SUBJECTS WILL KEEP THE REST UNDER OBSERVATION from a sense of duty, on the principle of volunteer service to the State. It will then be no disgrace to be a spy and informer, but a merit: unfounded denunciations, however, will be cruelly punished that there may be no development of abuses of this right.

Our agents will be taken from the higher as well as the lower ranks of society, from among the administrative class who spend their time in amusements, editors, printers and publishers, booksellers, clerks, and salesmen, workmen, coachmen, lackeys, etcetera. This body, having no rights and not being empowered to take any action on their own account, and consequently a police without any power, will only witness and report: verification of their reports and arrests will depend upon a responsible group of controllers of police affairs, while the actual act of arrest will be performed by the gendarmerie and the municipal police. Any person not denouncing anything seen or heard concerning questions of polity will also be charged with and made responsible for concealment, if it be proved that he is guilty of this crime.

JUST AS NOWADAYS OUR BRETHREN ARE OBLIGED AT THEIR OWN RISK TO DENOUNCE TO THE KABAL APOSTATES OF THEIR OWN FAMILY or members who have been noticed doing anything in opposition to the KABAL, SO IN OUR KINGDOM OVER ALL THE WORLD IT WILL BE OBLIGATORY FOR ALL OUR SUBJECTS TO OBSERVE THE DUTY OF SERVICE TO THE STATE IN THIS DIRECTION.

Such an organization will extirpate abuses of authority, of force, of bribery, everything in fact which we by our counsels, by our theories of the superhuman rights of man, have introduced into the customs of the goyim... But how else were we to procure that increase of causes predisposing to disorders in the midst of their administration?... Among the number of those methods one of the most important is -agents for the restoration of order, so placed as to have the opportunity in their disintegrating activity of developing and displaying their evil inclinations - obstinate self-conceit, irresponsible exercise of authority, and first and foremost, venality.

Protocol 18

Measures of secret defense. Observation of conspiracies from the inside. Overt secret defense - the ruin of authority. Secret defense of the King of the Jews. Mystical prestige of authority. Arrest on the first suspicion.

When it becomes necessary for us to strengthen the strict measures of secret defense (the most fatal poison for the prestige of authority) we shall arrange a simulation of disorders or some manifestation of discontents finding expression through the co-operation of good speakers. Round these speakers will assemble all who are sympathetic to his utterances. This will give us the pretext for domiciliary perquisitions and surveillance on the part of our servants from among the number of the GOYIM POLICE...

As the majority of the conspirators act out of love for the game, for the sake of talking, so, until they commit some overt act we shall not lay a finger on them but only introduce into their midst observation elements...

It must be remembered that the prestige of authority is lessened if it frequently discovers conspiracies against itself: this implies a presumption of consciousness of weakness, or, what is still worse, of injustice. You are aware that we have broken the prestige of the goy kings by frequent attempts upon their lives through our agents, blind sheep of our flock, who are easily moved by a few liberal phrases to crimes provided only they be painted in political colors. WE HAVE COMPELLED THE RULERS TO ACKNOWLEDGE THEIR WEAKNESS IN ADVERTISING OVERT MEASURES OF SECRET DEFENCE AND THEREBY WE SHALL BRING THE PROMISE OF AUTHORITY TO DESTRUCTION.

Our ruler will be secretly protected only by the most insignificant guard, because we shall not admit so much as a thought that there could exist

79

against him any sedition with which he is not strong enough to contend and is compelled to hide from it.

If we should admit this thought, as the goyim have done and are doing, we should IPSO FACTO be signing a death sentence, if not for our ruler, at any rate for his dynasty, at no distant date.

According to strictly enforced outward appearances our ruler will employ his power only for the advantage of the nation and in no wise for his own or dynastic profits. Therefore, with the observance of this decorum, his authority will be respected and guarded by the subjects themselves, it will receive an apotheosis in the admission that with it is bound up the well-being of every citizen of the State, for upon it will depend all order in the common life of the pack.

OVERT DEFENSE OF THE KING ARGUES WEAKNESS IN THE ORGANISATION OF HIS STRENGTH.

Our ruler will always among the people be surrounded by a mob of apparently curious men and women, who will occupy the front ranks about him, to all appearance by chance, and will restrain the ranks of the rest out of respect as it will appear for good order. This will sow an example of restraint also in others. If a petitioner appears among the people trying to hand a petition and forcing his way through the ranks, the first ranks must receive the petition and before the eyes of the petitioner pass it to the ruler, so that all may know that what is handed in reaches its destination, that, consequently, there exists a control of the ruler himself. The aureole of power requires for its existence that the people may be able to say: "If the king knew of this," or: "the king will hear of it."

WITH THE ESTABLISHMENT OF OFFICIAL SECRET DEFENSE THE MYSTICAL PRESTIGE OF AUTHORITY DISAPPEARS: given a certain audacity, and everyone counts himself master of it, the sedition-monger is conscious of his strength, and when occasion serves watches for the moment to make an attempt upon authority...

For the goyim we have been preaching something else, but by that very fact we are enabled to see what measures of overt defense have brought them to...

Criminals with us will be arrested at the first more or less well- grounded suspicion; it cannot be allowed that out of fear of a possible mistake an opportunity should be given of escape to persons suspected of a political lapse or crime, for in these matters we shall be literally merciless. If it is still possible, by stretching a point, to admit a reconsideration of the motive causes in simple crimes, there is no possibility of excuse for persons occupying themselves with questions in which nobody except the government can understand anything... And it is not all governments that understand true policy.

PROTOCOL 19

THE RIGHT OF PRESENTING PETITIONS AND PROJECTS. SEDITION. INDICTMENT OF POLITICAL CRIMES. ADVERTISEMENT OF POLITICAL CRIMES.

If we do not permit any independent dabbling in the political we shall on the other hand encourage every kind of report or petition with proposals for the government to examine into all kinds of projects for the amelioration of the condition of the people; this will reveal to us the defects or else the fantasies of our subjects, to which we shall respond either by accomplishing them or by a wise rebutting to prove the short-sightedness of one who judges wrongly.

Sedition-mongering is nothing more than the yapping of a lap-dog at an elephant. For a government well organized, not from the police but from the public point of view, the lap-dog yaps at the elephant in entire unconsciousness of its strength and importance. It needs no more than to take a good example to show the relative importance of both and the lap-dogs will cease to yap and will wag their tails the moment they set eyes on an elephant.

In order to destroy the prestige of heroism for political crime we shall send it for trial in the category of thieving, murder, and every kind of abominable and filthy crime. Public opinion will then confuse in its conception this category of crime with the disgrace attaching to every other and will brand it with the same contempt.

We have done our best, and I hope we have succeeded, to obtain that the goyim should not arrive at this means of contending with sedition. It was for this reason that through the press and in speeches, indirectly - in cleverly compiled schoolbooks on history, we have advertised the martyrdom alleged to have been accepted by sedition-mongers for the idea of the commonweal. This advertisement has increased the contingent of liberals and has brought thousands of goyim into the ranks of our livestock cattle.

PROTOCOL 20

FINANCIAL PROGRAMME. PROGRESSIVE TAX. STAMP PROGRESSIVE TAXATION. EXCHEQUER, INTEREST-BEARING PAPERS AND STAG- NATION OF CURRENCY. METHOD OF ACCOUNTING. CURRENCY ISSUE. GOLD STANDARD. STANDARD OF COST OF WORKING MAN POWER. BUDGET. STATE LOANS. ONE PER CENT. INTEREST SERIES. INDUSTRIAL SHARES. RULERS OF THE GOYIM: COURTIERS AND FAVORITISM. MASONIC AGENTS.

Today we shall touch upon the financial program, which I put off to the end of my report as being the most difficult, the crowning and the decisive point of our plans. Before entering upon it I will remind you that I have already spoken before by way of a hint when I said that the sum total of our actions is settled by the question of figures.

When we come into our kingdom our autocratic government will avoid, from a principle of self-preservation, sensibly burdening the masses of the people with taxes, remembering that it plays the part of father and protector. But as State organization costs dear it is necessary nevertheless to obtain the funds required for it. It will, therefore, elaborate with particular precaution the question of equilibrium in this matter.

Our rule, in which the king will enjoy the legal fiction that everything in his State belongs to him (which may easily be translated into fact), will be enabled to resort to the lawful confiscation of all sums of every kind for the regulation of their circulation in the State. From this follows that taxation will best be covered by a progressive tax on property. In this manner the dues will be paid without straitening or ruining anybody in the form of a percentage of the amount of property. The rich must be aware that it is their duty to place a part of their superfluities at the disposal of the State since the State guarantees them security of possession of the rest of their property and the right of honest gains, I say honest, for the control over property will do away with robbery on a legal basis.

This social reform must come from above, for the time is ripe for it - it is indispensable as a pledge of peace.

The tax upon the poor man is a seed of revolution and works to the detriment of the State which in hunting after the trifling is missing the big. Quite apart from this, a tax on capitalists diminishes the growth of wealth in private hands in which we have in these days concentrated it as a counterpoise to the government strength of the goyim - their State finances.

A tax increasing in a percentage ratio to capital will give a much larger revenue than the present individual or property tax, which is useful to us now for the sole reason that it excites trouble and discontent among the goyim.

The force upon which our king will rest consists in the equilibrium and the guarantee of peace, for the sake of which things it is indispensable that the capitalists should yield up a portion of their incomes for the sake of the secure working of the machinery of the State. State needs must be paid by those who will not feel the burden and have
enough to take from.

Such a measure will destroy the hatred of the poor man for the rich, in who he will see a necessary financial support for the State, will see in him the organizer of peace and well-being since he will see that it is the rich man who is paying the necessary means to attain these things.

In order that payers of the educated classes should not too much distress themselves over the new payments they will have full accounts given them of the destination of those payments, with the exception of such sums as will be appropriated for the needs of the throne and the administrative institutions.

He who reigns will not have any properties of his own once all in the State represents his patrimony, or else the one would be in contradiction to the other; the fact of holding private means would destroy the right of property in the common possessions of all.

Relatives of him who reigns, his heirs excepted, who will be maintained by the resources of the State, must enter the ranks of servants of the State or must work to obtain the right of property; the privilege of royal blood must not serve for the spoiling of the treasury.

Purchase, receipt of money or inheritance will be subject to the payment of a stamp progressive tax. Any transfer of property, whether money or other, without evidence of payment of this tax which will be strictly registered by names, will render the former holder liable to pat interest on the tax from the moment of transfer of these sums up to the discovery of his evasion of declaration of the transfer. Transfer documents must be presented weekly at the local treasury office with notification of the name, surname and permanent place of residence of the former and the new holder of the property. This transfer with register of names must begin from a definite sum which exceeds the ordinary expenses of buying and selling of necessaries, and these will be subject to payment only by a stamp impost of a definite percentage of the unit.

Just strike an estimate of how many times such taxes as these will cover the revenue of the GOYIM STATES.

The State exchequer will have to maintain a definite complement of reserve sums, and all that is collected above that complement must be returned into circulation. On these sums will be organized public works. The initiative of works of this kind, proceeding from State sources, will bind the working class family firmly to the interests of the State and to those who reign. From these same sums also a part will be set aside as rewards of inventiveness and productiveness.

On no account should so much as a single unit above the definite and freely estimated sums be retained in the State treasuries, for money exists to be circulated and any kind of stagnation of money acts ruinously on the running of the State machinery, for which it is the lubricant; a stagnation of the lubricant may stop the regular working of the mechanism.

The substitution of interest-bearing paper for a part of the token of exchange has produced exactly this stagnation. The consequences of this circumstance are already sufficiently noticeable.

A court of account will also be instituted by us and in it the ruler will find at any moment a full accounting for State income and expenditure, with the exception of the current monthly account, not yet made up, and that of the preceding month, which will not yet have been delivered.

The one and only person who will have no interest in robbing the State is its owner, the ruler. This is why his personal control will remove the possibility of leakages of extravagances.

The representative function of the ruler at receptions for the sake of etiquette, which absorbs so much invaluable time, will be abolished in order that the ruler may have time for control and consideration. His power will not then be split up into fractional parts among timeserving favorites who surround the throne for its pomp and splendor, and are interested only in their own and not in the common interests of the State.

Economic crises have been produced by us for the goyim by no other means than the withdrawal of money from circulation. Huge capitals have stagnated, withdrawing money from States, which were constantly obliged to apply to those same stagnant capitals for loans. These loans burdened the finances of the State with the payment of interest and made them the bond slaves of these capitals... The concentration of industry in the hands of capitalists out of the hands of small masters has drained away all the juices of the peoples and with them also the States...

The present issue of money in general does not correspond with the requirements per head, and cannot therefore satisfy all the needs of the workers. The issue of money ought to correspond with the growth of population and thereby children must also absolutely be reckoned as consumers of currency from the day of their birth. The revision of issue is a material question for the whole world.

YOU ARE AWARE THAT THE GOLD STANDARD HAS BEEN THE RUIN OF THE STATES WHICH ADOPTED IT, FOR IT HAS NOT BEEN ABLE TO SATIFSY THE DEMANDS FOR MONEY, THE MORE SO THAT WE HAVE REMOVED GOLD FROM CIRCULATION AS FAR AS POSSIBLE.

With us the standard that must be introduced is the cost of workingman power, whether it be reckoned in paper or in wood. We shall make the issue of money in accordance with the normal requirements of each subject, adding to the quantity with every birth and subtracting with every death.

The accounts will be managed by each department (the French administrative division), each circle.

In order that there may be no delays in the paying out of money for State needs the sums and terms of such payments will be fixed by decree of the ruler; this will do away with the protection by a ministry of one institution to the detriment of others.

The budgets of income and expenditures will be carried out side by side that they may not be obscured by distance one to another.

The reforms projected by us in the financial institutions and principles of the goyim will be closed by us in such forms will alarm nobody. We shall point out the necessity of reforms in consequence of the disorderly darkness into which the goyim by their irregularities have plunged the finances. The first irregularity, as we shall point out, consists in their beginning with drawing up a single budget which year after year grows owing to the following cause: this budget is dragged out to half the year, then they demand a budget to put things right, and this they expend in three months, after which they ask for a supplementary budget, and all this ends with a liquidation budget. But, as the budget of the following year is drawn up in accordance with the sum of the total addition, the annual departure from the normal reaches as much as 50 per cent. in a year, and so the annual budget is trebled in ten years. Thanks to such methods, allowed by the carelessness of the goy States, their treasuries are empty. The period of loans supervenes, and that has swallowed up remainders and brought all the goy States to bankruptcy.

You understand perfectly that economic arrangements of this kind, which have been suggested to the goyim by us, cannot be carried on by us.

Every kind of loan proves infirmity in the State and a want of understanding of the rights of the State. Loans hang like a sword of Damocles over the heads of rulers, who, instead of taking from their subjects by a temporary tax, come begging with outstretched palm of our bankers. Foreign loans are leeches which there is no possibility of removing from the body of the State until they fall off of themselves or the State flings them off. But the goy States do not tear them off; they go on in persisting in putting more on to themselves so that they must inevitably perish, drained by voluntary blood-letting.

What also indeed is, in substance, a loan, especially a foreign loan? A loan is - an issue of government bills of exchange containing a percentage obligation commensurate to the sum of the loan capital. If the loan bears a charge of 5 per cent., then in twenty years the State vainly pays away in interest a sum equal to the loan borrowed, in forty years it is paying a double sum, in sixty-treble, and all the while the debt remains an unpaid debt.

From this calculation it is obvious that with any form of taxation per head the State is baling out the last coppers of the poor taxpayers in order to settle accounts with wealthy foreigners, from whom it has borrowed money instead of collecting these coppers for its own needs without the additional interest.

So long as the loans were internal the goyim only shuffled their money from the pockets of the poor to those of the rich, but when we bought up the necessary person in order to transfer loans into the external sphere all the wealth of the States flowed into our cash-boxes and all the goyim began to pay us the tribute of subjects.

If the superficiality of goy kings on their thrones in regard to State affairs and the venality of ministers or the want of understanding of financial matters on the part of other ruling persons have made their countries debtors to our treasuries to amounts quite impossible to pay it has not been accomplished without on our part heavy expenditure of trouble and money.

Stagnation of money will not be allowed by us and therefore there will be no State interest-bearing paper, except at one per cent. series, so that there will be no payment of interest to leeches that suck all the strength out of the State. The right to issue interest-bearing paper will be given exclusively to industrial companies who will find no difficulty in paying interest out of profits, whereas the State does not make interest on borrowed money like these companies, for the State borrows to spend and not to use in operations.

Industrial papers will be bought also by the government which from being as now a payer of tribute by loan operations will be transformed into a lender of money at a profit. This measure will stop the stagnation of money, parasitic profits and idleness, all of which were useful for us among the goyim so long as they were independent but are not desirable under our rule.

How clear is the undeveloped power of thought of the purely brute brains of the goyim, as expressed in the fact that they have been borrowing from us with payment of interest without ever thinking that all the same these very moneys plus an addition for payment of interest must be got by them for their own State pockets in order to settle up with us. What could have been simpler than to take the money they wanted from their own people?

But it is a proof of the genius of our chosen mind that we have contrived to present the matter of loans to them in such a light that they have even seen in them an advantage for themselves.

Our accounts, which we shall present when the time comes, in the light of centuries of experience gained by experiments made by us on the goy States, will be distinguished by clearness and definiteness and will show at a glance to all men the advantage of our innovations. They will put an end to those abuses to which we owe our mastery over the goyim, but which cannot be allowed in our kingdom.

We shall so hedge about our system of accounting that neither the ruler nor the most insignificant public servant will be in a position to divert even the smallest sum from its destination without detection or to direct it in another direction except that which will be once fixed in a definite plan of action.

And without a definite plan it is impossible to rule. Marching along an undetermined road and with undetermined resources brings to ruin by the way heroes and semi-gods.

The goy rulers, whom we once upon a time advised should be distracted from State occupations by representative receptions, observances of etiquette, entertainments, were only screens for our rule. The accounts of favorite courtiers who replaced them in the sphere of affairs were drawn up for them by our agents, and every time gave satisfaction to short-sighted minds by promises that in the future economies and improvements were foreseen... Economies from what? From new taxes? - were questions that might have been but were not asked by those who read our accounts and projects...

You know to what they have been brought by this carelessness, to what a pitch of financial disorder they have arrived, notwithstanding the astonishing industry of their peoples...

Protocol 21

INTERNAL LOANS. DEBIT AND TAXES. CONVERSIONS. BANKRUPTCY. SAVINGS BANKS AND RENTES. ABOLITION OF MONEY MARKETS. REGULATION OF INDUSTRIAL VALUES.

To what I reported to you at the last meeting I shall now add a detailed explanation of external loans. Of foreign loans I shall say nothing more, because they have fed us with the national moneys of the goyim, but for our State there will be no foreigners, that is, nothing external.

We have taken advantage of the venality of administrators and the slackness of rulers to get our moneys twice, thrice and more times over, by lending to the goy governments moneys which were not at all needed by the States. Could anyone do the like in regard to us?... Therefore, I shall only deal with the details of internal loans.

States announce that such a loan is to be concluded and open subscriptions for their own bills of exchange, that is, for their interest bearing paper. That they may be within the reach of all the price is determined at from a hundred to a thousand; and a discount is made for the earliest subscribers. Next day by artificial means the price of them goes up, the alleged reason being that everyone is rushing to buy them. In a few days the treasury safes are as they say overflowing and there's more money than they can do with (why then take it?). The subscription, it is alleged, covers many times over the issue total of the loan; in this lies the whole stage effect - look you, they say, what confidence is shown in the government's bills of exchange.

But when the comedy is played out there emerges the fact that a debit and an exceedingly burdensome debit has been created. For the payment of interest it becomes necessary to have recourse to new loans, which do not swallow up but only add to the capital debt. And when this credit is exhausted it becomes necessary by new taxes to cover, not the loan, but only the interest on it. These taxes are a debit employed to cover a debit...

Later comes the time for conversions, but they diminish the payment of interest without covering the debt, and besides they cannot be made without the consent of the lenders; on announcing a conversion a proposal is made to return the money to those who are not willing to convert their paper. If everybody expressed his unwillingness and demanded his money back, the government would be hooked on their own flies and would be found insolvent and unable to pay the proposed sums. By good luck the subjects of the goy governments, knowing nothing about financial affairs, have always preferred losses on exchange and diminution of interest to the risk of new investments of their moneys, and have thereby many a time enabled these governments to throw off their shoulders a debit of several millions.

Nowadays, with external loans, these tricks cannot be played by the goyim for they know that we shall demand all our moneys back.

In this way an acknowledged bankruptcy will best prove to the various countries the absence of any means between the interests of the peoples and those who rule them.

I beg you to concentrate your particular attention upon this point and upon the following: nowadays all internal loans are consolidated by so-called flying loans, that is, such as have terms of payments more or less near. These debts consist of moneys paid into the savings banks and reserve funds. If left for long at the disposition of a government these funds evaporate in the payment of interest on foreign loans, and are replaced by the deposit of equivalent amount of RENTES.

And these last it is which patch up all the leaks in the State treasuries of the goyim.

When we ascend the throne of the world all these financial and similar shifts, as being not in accord with our interests, will be swept away so as not to leave a trace, as also will be destroyed all money markets, since we will not allow the prestige of our power to be shaken by fluctuations of prices set upon our values, which we shall announce by law at the price which represents their full worth without any possibility of lowering or raising. (Raising gives the pretext for lowering, which indeed was where we made a beginning in relation to the values of the goyim.)

We shall replace the money markets by grandiose government credit institutions, the object of which will be to fix the price of industrial values in accordance with government views. These institutions will be in a position to fling upon the market five hundred millions of industrial paper in one day, or to buy up for the same amount. In this way all industrial undertakings will come into dependence upon us. You may imagine for yourselves what immense power we shall thereby secure for ourselves... .

Protocol 22

In all that has so far been reported by me to you, I have endeavored to depict with care the secret of what is coming, of what is past, and of what is going on now, rushing into the flood of the great events coming already in the near future, the secret of our relations to the goyim and of financial operations. On this subject there remains still a little for me to add.

IN OUR HANDS IS THE GREATEST POWER OF OUR DAY - GOLD: IN TWO DAYS WE CAN PRODUCE FROM OUR STOREHOUSES ANY QUANTITY WE MAY PLEASE.

Surely there is no need to seek further proof that our rule is predestined by God? Surely we shall not fail with such wealth to prove that all that evil which for so many centuries we have had to commit has served at the end of ends the cause of true well-being - the bringing of everything into order? Though it even be by the exercise of some violence, yet all the same it will be established. We shall contrive to prove that we are benefactors who have restored to the rent and mangled earth the true good and also freedom of the person, and therewith we shall enable it to be enjoyed in peace and quiet, with proper dignity of relations, on the condition of course, of strict observance of the laws established by us. We shall make plain therewith that freedom does not consist in dissipation and in the right of unbridled license any more than dignity and force of a man do not consist in the right for everyone to promulgate destructive principles in the nature of freedom of conscience, equality and the like, that freedom of the person in no wise consists in the right to agitate oneself and others by abominable speeches before disorderly mobs, and that true freedom consists in the inviolability of the person who honorably and strictly observes all the laws of life in common, that human

97

dignity is wrapped up in consciousness of the rights and also of the absence of rights of each, and not wholly and solely in fantastic imaginings about the subject of one's ego.

Our authority will be glorious because it will be all-powerful, will rule and guide, and not muddle along after leaders and orators shrieking themselves hoarse with senseless words which they call great principles and which are nothing else, to speak honestly, but utopian... Our authority will be the crown of order, and in that is included the whole happiness of man. The aureole of this authority will inspire a mystical bowing of the knee before it and a reverent fear before it of all the peoples. True force makes no terms with any right, not even with that of God: none dare come near to it so as to take so much as a span from it away. .

PROTOCOL 23

REDUCTION OF THE MANUFACTURE OF ARTICLES OF LUXURY. SMALL MASTER PRODUCTION. UNEMPLOYMENT. PROHIBITION OF DRUNKENESS. KILLING OUT OF THE OLD SOCIETY AND ITS RESURRECTION IN A NEW FORM. THE CHOSEN ONE OF GOD.

That the peoples may become accustomed to obedience it is necessary to inculcate lessons of humility and therefore to reduce the production of articles of luxury. By this we shall improve morals which have been debased by emulation in the sphere of luxury. We shall re-establish small master production which will mean laying a mine under the private capital of manufacturers. This is indispensable also for the reason that manufacturers on the grand scale often move, though not always consciously, the thoughts of the masses in directions against the government. A people of small masters knows nothing of unemployment and this binds him closely with existing order, and consequently with the firmness of authority. Unemployment is a most perilous thing for a government. For us its part will have been played out the moment authority is transferred into our hands. Drunkenness also will be prohibited by law and punishable as a crime against the humanness of man who is turned into a brute under the influence of alcohol.

Subjects, I repeat once more, give blind obedience only to the strong hand which is absolutely independent of them, for in it they feel the sword of defense and support against social scourges... What do they want with an angelic spirit in a king? What they have to see in him is the personification of force and power.

The supreme lord who will replace all now existing rulers, dragging on their existence among societies demoralized by us, societies that have denied even the authority of God, from whose midst breaks out on all sides the fire of anarchy, must first of all proceed to quench this all-devouring flame. Therefore he will be obliged to kill off those existing societies, though he should drench them with his own blood, that he may resurrect them again in the form of regularly organized troops fighting consciously with every kind of infection that may cover the body of the State with sores.

This Chosen One of God is chosen from above to demolish the senseless forces moved by instinct and not reason, by brutishness and not humanness. These forces now triumph in manifestations of robbery and every kind of violence under the mask of principles of freedom and rights. They have overthrown all forms of social order to erect on the ruins the throne of the King of the Jews; but their part will be played out the moment he enters into his kingdom. Then it will be necessary to sweep them away from his path, on which must be left no knot, no splinter.

Then will it be possible for us to say to the peoples of the world: "Give thanks to God and bow the knee before him who bears on his front the seal of the predestination of man, to which God Himself has led his star that none other but He might free us from all the before-mentioned forces and evils."

PROTOCOL 24

CONFIRMING THE ROOTS OF KING DAVID (?). TRAINING OF
THE KING. SETTING ASIDE OF DIRECT HEIRS. THE KING
AND THREE OF HIS SPONSORS. THE KING IS FATE.
IRREPROACHABILITY OF EXTERIOR MORALITY OF THE KING
OF THE JEWS.

I pass now to the method of confirming the dynastic roots of King
David to the last strata of the earth.

This confirmation will first and foremost be included in that in which
to this day has rested the force of conservatism by our learned elders of
the conduct of all the affairs of the world, in the directing of the education
of thought of all humanity.

Certain members of the seed of David will prepare the kings and their
heirs, selecting not by right of heritage but by eminent capacities,
inducting them into the most secret mysteries of the political, into
schemes of government, but providing always that none may come to
knowledge of the secrets. The object of this mode of action is that all may
know that government cannot be entrusted to those who have not been
inducted into the secret places of its art...

To these persons only will be taught the practical application of the
afore-named plans by comparison of the experiences of many centuries,
all the observations on the politico-economic moves and social sciences -
in a word, all the spirit of laws which have been unshakably established by
nature herself for the regulation of the relations of humanity.

Direct heirs will often be set aside from ascending the throne if in their
time of training they exhibit frivolity, softness and other qualities that are the
ruin of authority, which render them incapable of governing and in
themselves dangerous for kingly office.

Only those who are unconditionally capable for firm, even if it be to
cruelty, direct rule will receive the reins of rule from our learned elders.

In case of falling sick with weakness of will or other form of incapacity, kings must by law hand over the reins of rule to new and capable hands...

The king's plan of action for the current moment, and all the more so for the future, will be unknown, even to those who are called his closest counselors.

Only the king and the three who stood sponsor for him will know what is coming.

In the person of the king who with unbending will is master of himself and of humanity all will discern as it were fate with its mysterious ways. None will know what the king wishes to attain by his dispositions, and therefore none will dare to stand across an unknown path.

It is understood that the brain reservoir of the king must correspond in capacity to the plan of government it has to contain. It is for this reason that he will ascend the throne not otherwise than after examination of his mind by the aforesaid learned elders.

That the people may know and love their king it is indispensable for him to converse in the market-places with his people. This ensures the necessary clinching of the two forces which are now divided one from another by us by the terror.

This terror was indispensable for us till the time comes for both these forces separately to fall under our influence.

The King of the Jews must not be at the mercy of his passions, and especially of sensuality: on no side of his character must he give brute instincts power over his mind. Sensuality worse than all else disorganizes the capacities of the mind and clearness of views, distracting the thoughts to the worst and most brutal side of human activity.

The prop of humanity in the person of the supreme lord of all the world of the holy seed of David must sacrifice to his people all personal inclinations. Our supreme lord must be of an exemplary irreproachability.

www.ingramcontent.com/pod-product-compliance
Lightning Source LLC
Chambersburg PA
CBHW071619040426
42452CB00009B/1403

*9 7 8 1 6 0 9 4 2 0 2 3 9 *